THE CANNING KITCHEN

THE CANNING KITCHEN

101 SIMPLE SMALL BATCH RECIPES

AMY BRONEE

PENGUIN

an imprint of Penguin Canada Books Inc., a Penguin Random House Company

Published by the Penguin Group

Penguin Canada Books Inc., 90 Eglinton Avenue East, Suite 700, Toronto, Ontario, Canada M4P 2Y3

Penguin Group (USA) LLC, 375 Hudson Street, New York, New York 10014, U.S.A.

Penguin Books Ltd, 80 Strand, London WC2R 0RL, England

Penguin Ireland, 25 St Stephen's Green, Dublin 2, Ireland (a division of Penguin Books Ltd)

Penguin Group (Australia), 707 Collins Street, Melbourne, Victoria 3008, Australia (a division of Pearson Australia Group Pty Ltd)

Penguin Books India Pvt Ltd, 11 Community Centre, Panchsheel Park, New Delhi – 110 017, India

Penguin Group (NZ), 67 Apollo Drive, Rosedale, Auckland 0632, New Zealand (a division of Pearson New Zealand Ltd)

Penguin Books (South Africa) (Pty) Ltd, 24 Sturdee Avenue, Rosebank, Johannesburg 2196, South Africa

Penguin Books Ltd, Registered Offices: 80 Strand, London WC2R 0RL, England

First published 2015

1 2 3 4 5 6 7 8 9 10

Manufactured in China

LIBRARY AND ARCHIVES CANADA CATALOGUING IN PUBLICATION

Bronee, Amy, author
    The canning kitchen : 101 simple small batch recipes / Amy Bronee.

Includes index.
ISBN 978-0-14-319131-5 (pbk.)

    1. Canning and preserving. 2. Cookbooks. I. Title.

TX603.B79 2015   641.4'2   C2015-900346-6

Visit the Penguin Canada website at www.penguin.ca

Special and corporate bulk purchase rates available; please see www.penguin.ca/corporatesales or call 1-800-810-3104.

FOR RUE AND HIS DADVENTURES
THAT MADE IT POSSIBLE FOR ME
TO WRITE THIS BOOK.

CONTENTS

INTRODUCTION

The sound of knives clinking in jars was standard dinner music in my childhood. The fridge door was heavy with jarred flavours, and on barbecue night they all came out to take up residence in the middle of the dinner table. It was that mixing and matching of flavours that began my lifelong love of preserves. Now, through my food blog FamilyFeedbag.com and my hands-on cooking classes, I get to share my love of canning with other home cooks and demystify the process of preserving fresh food in jars. It's this connection with other home cooks through writing and teaching that keeps me motivated and inspired in my own kitchen.

While I also adore making classic comfort foods like stews and pies, one of the most pleasurable ways I spend time in the kitchen is filling jars with homemade jams, jellies, marmalades, pickles, relishes, chutneys and sweet and savoury staples. There's nothing like getting out my canning supplies and chopping up fresh seasonal ingredients with music swirling above my head to remind me that my favourite place on earth really is my happy little kitchen. This book is an invitation into my canning kitchen so I can share with you some of my favourite homemade preserves.

People can food for many different reasons. For some it's about preserving a connection to our past or preserving freshness that's in season to enjoy another day. For some it's about making a jam or salsa that isn't in stores, or knowing exactly what goes into your food. For others it's simply about spending time, apron on and knife in hand, crafting something beautiful to share. Most often for me, making jam with strawberries from my own garden or jelly with apples from my own tree, it is about slowing down to live in the past and the right now at the very same time. Every glossy jar cooling on the counter represents contentment for me; regardless of whatever is going on out there in the world, everything is just as it should be in my kitchen.

It's a joy for me to help home cooks discover how surprisingly simple canning is. Any home kitchen can become a canning kitchen with the use of a few tools, some of which you may already have. With time you will find your own unique rhythm and method for filling jars with delicious homemade preserves. Whether you're new to preserving or an experienced home canner, the simple instructions in this book will lead you to delicious results with every batch.

This book blends the traditions of the canning kitchen with the tastes of the modern kitchen. I'm sharing my much-loved classics like strawberry jam and crunchy dill pickles alongside recipes for exciting new classics like delicious barbecue sauces, beverage concentrates and interesting mustards. You'll find recipes inspired by flavours from the traditional to the international, including the tastes of Mexico, India, China, Thailand and more. With ideas for fresh ingredients in every season, you'll want to keep your canning pot handy year-round.

In these pages, I hope you find the tasty things, the sticky things, the sweet and the savoury things that you'll enjoy making in your own canning kitchen for years to come.

Enjoy.

Canning Kitchen Basics

Canning is easier than you might think, and once you get started making your own delicious preserves, it's hard to stop. The sight of sealed jars cooling on the kitchen counter is deeply satisfying, and suddenly you're buying fresh produce by the case and giving away jars of homemade jams as gifts just so you can make more. However, new and experienced canners alike are often filled with questions about filling jars. To boost your canning confidence, here are the simple answers to some common questions about making your own preserves.

Do I need a lot of equipment?

Most of what you need to make your home kitchen a canning kitchen you may already own. The key piece of equipment is a canning pot with a rack and lid for processing your filled jars. You can either buy an inexpensive speckled enamel canner with a rack where canning supplies are sold, or find a rack to fit a large stockpot you already own. Other tools, both necessary and just nice to have, are discussed in the Canning Kitchen Equipment section (page 11).

How much time does it take to can something?

The time it takes to prepare a recipe varies. Jams and pickles often come together quickly with few ingredients, whereas relishes and chutneys generally involve more preparation. Some people love spending time in the kitchen with a knife and cutting board with some music playing, while others like to make use of a food processor to speed up preparation time. The choice is yours.

The processing time also varies with each recipe, ranging from 10 minutes to as long as 40 minutes. Experienced canners can make a batch of jam in about half an hour from start to finish. However long it takes you, the results are always worth it.

How does canning work?

Two key things happen when a filled jar is submerged under boiling water. First, the high temperature kills off any yeasts, moulds or bacteria in the food that can cause spoilage. Second, the contents of the jar expand, driving out air. As the jar cools, the contents contract, causing the lid to seal and preventing any new microorganisms from entering the jar during storage.

It's important to follow the headspace recommendation for each recipe. The headspace is the gap between the surface of the food and the rim of the jar. Some foods expand more than others during processing, and the proper headspace helps each jar to form a strong vacuum seal. An inexpensive headspace measuring tool can help you check for accuracy.

The stated processing time should also be followed carefully, as some higher-density foods such as whole tomatoes and apricot halves, as well as foods near the acid/low-acid pH borderline, need a longer processing time. Jar size also plays a role in processing times, so use the jar size recommended in each recipe.

Do I have to sterilize my jars before filling them?

No, not for the recipes in this book. Current North American home canning guidelines from the United States Department of Agriculture and the National Center for Home Food Preservation state that canning jars do not need to be sterilized if they will be processed in a boiling water bath canner for 10 minutes or longer. Since all the recipes in this book are processed for at least 10 minutes, you do not need to sterilize your jars before you fill them. However, it is important to start with spotlessly clean jars that have been washed in hot soapy water and left to air-dry or washed in the dishwasher on a normal wash cycle.

Jar sterilization was standard for the old open kettle canning method, in which the filled jars would be left to seal on their own without further processing. The open kettle method, as well as the oven canning method, are not recommended by North American food safety agencies because these methods may not achieve high enough temperatures to kill microorganisms that can cause food spoilage.

Can I reuse jars and lids?

Jars can be reused indefinitely as long as they are in good shape. Check for chips and scratches before reusing, as damaged jars may not form a vacuum seal and can break during processing. Screw bands can be reused as long as they are free of rust and dents. Flat lids, however, should be used only once because the sealing compound can't be relied on to form a seal more than once. Flat lids can be purchased in boxes of a dozen or more.

What is the difference between boiling water bath canning and pressure canning?

Boiling water bath canning, which involves boiling filled jars under water for a specified time, is safe for acid foods and mixtures with a pH of 4.6 or lower, such as fruit jams, fruit jellies, chutneys, relishes, pickles and tomatoes with adequate acidity from added lemon juice, vinegar or citric acid. Pressure canning, which uses a lockable pot with vents to control pressure, must be used for canning low-acid foods (those with a pH higher than 4.6), such as meats, poultry, fish and vegetables. This book contains boiling water bath canning recipes only, since all the recipes are for acid foods or mixtures with a pH of 4.6 or lower.

Can canned food be dangerous?

Boiling water bath canning is very safe if you follow current canning guidelines and a trusted recipe. The only foods that should be boiling water bath canned are acid foods such as fruit jams, fruit jellies, marmalades, pickles, chutneys, relishes and other acid mixtures at or below 4.6 pH. Botulism, caused by the soil-based bacterium *Clostridium botulinum*, is serious. The spores are heat-resistant and grow in moist low-acid, low-oxygen environments. You can safely use boiling water bath canning for all the recipes in this book because they are all for acid foods and mixtures.

Just as with fresh food, proper storage is important to prevent foodborne illness. Before storing your processed jars, allow them to cool completely, then check for a good seal by pressing down on the middle of the lid. If the centre of the lid is down and stays concave when pressed, the jar has sealed and the contents are safe to keep at room temperature for up to 1 year. If the centre of the lid pops up and down when pressed, or if the lid moves in any way, the jar hasn't sealed. An unsealed jar should be stored in the refrigerator and consumed first.

Do I have to work in large batches?

Not at all. In fact, most jams require only about 3 lb (1.4 kg) of fruit, resulting in about half a dozen 250 mL (1 cup) jars at a time. Other recipes, such as chutneys, relishes and sauces, usually contain more ingredients in slightly larger volumes. The recipes in this book are designed to leave you with just enough jars to make your efforts worthwhile and have a couple of jars extra to share or give away as gifts.

To keep costs low, use ingredients when they are in season at good prices. Buy directly from farmers and visit U-picks. Ingredients can even be free. Ask a friend or neighbour if you can pick their untended fruit trees in exchange for some of the delicious preserves you'll make. With a little space, you can even start your very own canning kitchen garden, growing things like pickling cucumbers, tomatoes, rhubarb and strawberries.

If I want to make more, can I double a recipe?

It depends what type of preserves you are making. Jams, jellies and marmalades should always be made in small batches, as they require adequate surface area for evaporation and can bubble up to double their volume while cooking. Similarly, recipes that require a longer cooking time, such as chutneys, fruit butters and barbecue sauces, may not achieve adequate reduction and flavour concentration in large batches. Generally, pickles and relishes can be safely doubled.

What is pectin?

Often mistaken for a preservative or an animal-based product (that's gelatin), pectin is a naturally occurring fibre found in most plant cells. Pectin is activated when it's combined with sugar in an acid mixture over high heat, producing a gel set for jams and jellies. Some fruits, such as strawberries and peaches, contain very little pectin, while other fruits, such as apples and citrus, have a lot of pectin concentrated in their seeds and skins.

Commercially available pectin is the by-product of citrus and apple juice production. The leftover pomace is processed, dried and milled into fine crystals. Although it is possible to make jams and jellies without added pectin, no-added-pectin jams and jellies can require cooking times of up to four times longer, which may cook the flavour and joy out of your fresh ingredients. Many of the jam and jelly recipes in this book use added pectin and a short cooking time to lock in the natural fresh fruit flavour, colour and texture. Where best results are achieved using the naturally occurring pectin in the ingredients, no pectin is added in the recipe.

The recipes in this book call for regular pectin powder. Commercial pectins come in powdered and liquid form, and they are not interchangeable. Generally, powdered pectins are added early in the recipe, whereas liquid pectins are added near the end. The two forms can also require different amounts of sugar to create a gel set. I prefer to use powdered pectin because it usually comes at a better price, which is nice when I'm making a lot of preserves. Pectins also come in low-sugar and no-sugar varieties for making jams and jellies with little or no added sugar or with other sweeteners. These other powdered pectins are not suitable for the traditional jams in this book.

How do I make sure my jams, jellies and marmalades will set?

Since jams, jellies and marmalades are hot and liquid when they are ladled into jars, it can be tricky to tell if they will set in a spreadable gel texture once cooled. Newer jam makers sometimes try to leave out some of the sugar in the recipe or fail to boil their preserves hard enough. Both these mistakes can lead to gel failure. By following the instructions carefully and using the right ingredients in the suggested amounts, you will be able to make the preserves of your dreams.

How to test a gel set

The freezer plate test—Keep a small plate cold in the freezer. To test your hot preserves, spoon a small amount onto the cold plate and return it to the freezer. After 1 minute, remove the plate from the freezer and poke a finger into the preserve. If it wrinkles slightly, it will gel when it cools. If it doesn't wrinkle, continue boiling on full heat, testing again every 1 to 2 minutes until it passes the freezer plate test.

The spoon sheeting test—Dip a metal spoon into your cooked preserves. Hold the spoon over the pot and watch it carefully. If your preserve slides off in a sheet, it is ready to ladle into jars. If it falls off the spoon in wet drips, continue boiling on full heat, testing again every 1 to 2 minutes until it passes the spoon sheeting test.

How do I get crystal-clear jellies like I see at farmers' markets and country fairs?

Starting with a clear fruit juice is the first step to a clear jelly. Straining off cooked fruit with a jelly bag will remove tiny fruit particles from the juice that could cloud your jelly. Also, when many fruit preserves are boiled, they foam up a lot and develop a fruit scum on the surface. Skimming off this scum results in the clearest jellies, but it can be tricky to get it all. Before filling jars, use a wooden spoon to drag the scum gently across the surface toward you, then scoop it from the edge of the pot. If you don't get it all, not to worry. A little left behind doesn't affect the overall flavour of your preserves.

Can I make substitutions?

Yes and no. When it comes to main ingredients and their ratios, use what is stated in the recipe to ensure safe acid levels. Since canning is all about safe acid levels, follow the acidification amounts in the recipe. If you'd like to substitute red wine vinegar for cider vinegar, for example, be sure to always use vinegars with at least 5% acetic acid (the label will state the percentage). Experimenting with various spices, such as ground allspice instead of ground cinnamon, is also fine. Some of these substitutions and additions are suggested in the recipes.

I've heard that overripe produce is perfect for canning. Is this true?

Your preserves are only as good as the ingredients you start with. For the tastiest results, choose fresh fruit and vegetables at their peak, as well as fresh spices. The exception is recipes that call for bottled lemon juice to ensure safe acid levels. Bottled lemon juice has a standardized acid level, whereas the acidity of fresh lemons can vary depending on ripeness and length of storage.

Can I use frozen fruit to make jams and jellies?

Stock up on fresh food in season and freeze for canning another day when those ingredients are harder to find. Generally, foods that freeze well, such as rhubarb, peaches and berries, are reliable choices for freezing to make jams and jellies later on. It is a good idea to weigh or measure ingredients before freezing, so you know you have the right amount for the recipe you want to make. Wash food first, and when it's frozen, store in bags or containers designed for freezer use. Label foods with the amount and date and use within 6 months. Allow frozen fruit to thaw completely before using, and don't drain off any juices.

How long will my preserves last?

Home-canned preserves are safe to store at room temperature for up to 1 year. Clearly label your sealed jars with the contents and date, and store in a cool spot, with or without the screw bands. Excessive sunlight can discolour some preserves, so choose a spot away from windows. Once opened, store your delicious preserves in the refrigerator. Don't consume any preserves that look or smell off or if the lid has become unsealed. When in doubt, throw it out.

How does altitude affect the canning process?

Canning at higher altitudes requires a longer processing time because of differences in atmospheric pressure. Water boils at a lower temperature as altitude rises, and lower temperatures are less effective at killing bacteria that can lead to food spoilage. Longer processing times at higher elevations make up for the lower temperature. If you don't know what altitude you live at, check online or call your regional geological survey office. Adjust processing times as follows if you are preserving at altitudes over 1,000 feet (305 metres) above sea level.

Elevation above sea level	Timing adjustment
Up to 1,000 feet (305 metres)	Use processing time in recipe
1,001–3,000 feet (306–914 metres)	Add 5 minutes to processing time in recipe
3,001–6,000 feet (915–1829 metres)	Add 10 minutes to processing time in recipe
6,001–8,000 feet (1830–2438 metres)	Add 15 minutes to processing time in recipe
8,001–10,000 feet (2439–3048 metres)	Add 20 minutes to processing time in recipe

*Data source: National Center for Home Food Preservation

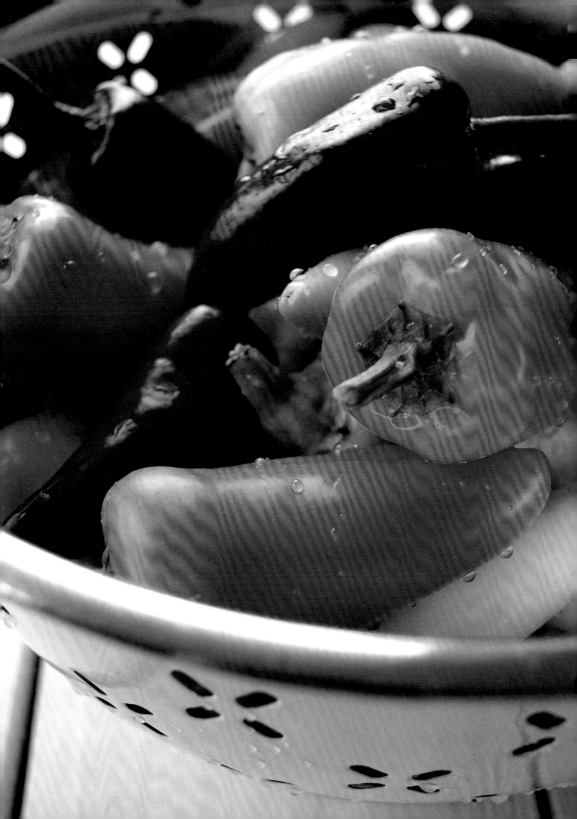

Canning Kitchen Equipment

Any home kitchen can become a canning kitchen with the addition of a few simple tools. Which tools you will need depends on what you're canning and how you prefer to set up your space. Over time you will find your own rhythm and method for preserving food in jars. Some people prefer tools like food processors and electric citrus juicers to speed things along, while others enjoy the ritual of preparing ingredients with a simple knife and cutting board.

Here's an overview of the equipment commonly used in a canning kitchen. Look for these items at hardware stores, kitchen stores or wherever canning supplies are sold. Some of them are must-haves, some are needed for certain recipes, and others are just nice to have. You will already have many of these tools at home.

MUST HAVE

Boiling water bath canner

Any large, deep pot with a lid can be used as a boiling water bath canner, as long as you have a rack to keep jars raised slightly off the bottom. Classic speckled enamel canners, which often come with a fitted rack and other canning tools, are inexpensive and easily found year-round in most hardware stores. If you want something that can double as a stockpot, choose a canning rack first, then find any large, deep pot with a lid that your rack will fit inside.

Canning rack

Filled jars should be held slightly off the bottom of the canning pot while boiling (processing) to maintain adequate water circulation for even heat distribution and to prevent jars from breaking. Racks are usually made of metal with contoured handles that rest on the canner's rim for easy lowering and removal of jars from the boiling water. Racks made of heat-resistant plastic are also available. While most mason jars will fit in any canning rack, some racks are better suited to certain jar sizes. A flat wire rack, rather than a contoured one, will fit all jar sizes nicely.

Chef's knife and large cutting board

These two tools will play a part in almost every canning recipe you make, but that doesn't mean they have to be pricey. I prefer an 8-inch (20 cm) chef's knife, but it's important to choose a sharp knife you feel comfortable using. If you take care of your knives they will take care of you, so learn to use a sharpening steel to keep your knives slicing cleanly and safely. If your cutting board slides around on the kitchen counter, slip a dampened dish towel or paper towel underneath to hold it steady.

Jars

Mason jars with either a standard or a wide-mouth opening are the most popular jar for home canning. Designed to hold up under high heat and fit a two-piece screw-on lid, they are commonly available year-round wherever canning supplies are sold. Several brands are available and they come in the standard sizes of 125 mL (½ cup), 250 mL (1 cup), 500 mL (2 cup) and 1 L (4 cup), although larger sizes are available. They are mostly sold in cases of a dozen jars, but patterned or interestingly shaped jars are also available in smaller quantities per package and usually for a higher price per jar. Do not use jars that are not designed for home canning.

Mason jars can be reused indefinitely, but always check for cracks and chips, as these can interfere with a good seal or can lead to breakage during processing. Jars do not need to be sterilized before filling if they will be processed in a boiling water bath canner for 10 minutes or longer. Since all the recipes in this book are processed for at least 10 minutes, you do not need to sterilize your jars before you fill them. However, they should be spotlessly cleaned by washing in hot soapy water and left to air-dry or washed in the dishwasher on a normal wash cycle.

Ladle

Using a ladle is the safest way to move hot liquids from a hot pot to hot jars. Since you'll be working at very high temperatures, be sure to use a ladle that is made of a heat-resistant material such as stainless steel.

Large, heavy-bottomed pot with a lid

Most of the recipes you put into jars to process will be cooked first. A large pot—one that can hold about 8 quarts (7.5 L)—will work for everything in this book, from jams, jellies and marmalades to pickles, relishes and chutneys. Use a pot that has a heavy, or thickened, bottom that will promote even heat distribution and help prevent scorching. Acidic ingredients like citrus and vinegar will discolour pots made of aluminum, tin or copper, so choose a nonreactive material such as stainless steel or enamel.

Lids

Self-sealing two-piece lids consisting of a flat lid and a screw-on band are the gold standard for home canning. Flat lids have a gasket compound on the underside, which is soft enough when hot to allow air to escape during processing. As the contents of a jar cool and shrink slightly, a vacuum is formed, pulling the lid down to form an airtight seal. This prevents any new microorganisms from entering the jar and spoiling the food during storage. Screw bands can be reused if they are undented and rust-free, but the flat lids are a single-use item. Two-piece lids come in both standard and wide-mouth sizes. Follow the manufacturer's instructions on the package to prepare lids for processing.

Measuring cups and spoons

Since canning requires some level of accuracy, measuring cups and spoons are useful tools to keep within grabbing reach in your canning kitchen. A clear 2-cup (500 mL) or 4-cup (1 L) measuring cup with a marked scale plus a few smaller measuring cups—¼-cup (60 mL), ⅓-cup (75 mL) and ½-cup (125 mL)—plus a set of measuring spoons will do the trick.

MUST HAVE FOR SOME RECIPES
Blender

Some canning recipes require puréed fruits or vegetables, and a blender makes the job quick and easy. Use a standard countertop blender if you prefer, or an immersion blender right in the pot. A food mill is a good substitute for a blender when puréeing cooked foods. When working with raw foods, a blender is the best choice. A food processor, while useful for finely chopping, doesn't achieve a true purée.

Cheesecloth

Particularly useful for making marmalades, inexpensive cheesecloth is used to form a pouch for high-pectin citrus peels and seeds that can be submerged while cooking and easily discarded afterward. Cheesecloth is also handy for draining and squeezing out excess moisture from salted vegetables when making relish. Look for cheesecloth at any hardware store, kitchen store or even a dollar store. Washable muslin can be used in place of cheesecloth.

Jelly bag

Straining boiled fruit through a jelly bag is the first step in getting the clearest jewel-like jellies. The bag is suspended over a bowl to catch the drips, using a special stand or suspended from kitchen cabinet handles with a sturdy elastic. Washable and reusable, jelly bags are commonly available wherever canning supplies are sold. A colander lined with a double layer of water-dampened cheesecloth can double as a jelly bag.

Kitchen string

Cotton kitchen string transforms a square of cheesecloth into a pouch for adding flavour and natural pectin from citrus peels and seeds to preserves while cooking. Don't substitute yarn or other coloured fibres, as the dyes may run. For a truly secure pouch, use a double layer of cheesecloth with a double knot of kitchen string.

Masher

That masher you use for making fluffy mashed potatoes is also the most effective tool for crushing berries and other soft fruits for jams, dessert sauces and other preserves. Crushing by hand, as opposed to chopping in a food processor, allows you to stop at just the right consistency.

Peeler

Using a potato or vegetable peeler is a quick alternative to peeling with a knife. Whether it's inexpensive or pricey, straight or Y-shaped, choose one that feels good in your hand. Peelers do get dull over time, so it's a good idea to replace your peeler when it isn't working as well as it once did.

Wooden spoon

While silicone and metal spoons will stir jams and chutneys just fine, there's nothing quite like the traditional simplicity of a wooden spoon to feel your way through a batch of preserves. A wooden spoon is also the ideal tool for skimming fruit scum off your cooked preserves before ladling them into jars, and the handle end is useful for stirring tender sliced fruits in light syrup without damaging them.

NICE TO HAVE
Canning funnel

A canning funnel is a handy and inexpensive tool that can speed up your canning. With a wide opening at the bottom that fits inside the rim of a jar, a canning funnel will help you get your delicious jams, jellies and other goodies inside your jars rather than down the sides of them.

Citrus juicer

Since citrus fruits are a common ingredient in canning recipes and are often processed in abundance, an effective tool for juicing citrus is handy to have. Either an electric citrus juicer or a manual reamer will save a significant amount of prep time and result in getting more juice from your fruit than squeezing by hand.

Food mill

Sometimes you want to use the fruit peels during cooking but don't want them in the finished product. For example, applesauce takes on a beautiful rosy pink colour when the apple skins are left on during cooking. Running the cooked sauce through a food mill will purée the sauce while catching the skins so they can be discarded. A conical sieve, also called a chinois, with a wooden dowel to push the food through performs the same task.

Food processor

While not necessary in the canning kitchen, a food processor sure can speed things along when you're prepping a lot of ingredients, particularly with finely chopped relishes. Look for one with a large bowl and sturdy parts from a brand you trust.

Headspace measuring tool/bubble remover

Poke one end of this plastic tool into your jars of relishes, chutneys and other chunky preserves to remove any air bubbles before processing. The jagged edge at the other end allows you to measure headspace—the gap between the surface of the food and the rim of the jar—in graduated ¼-inch (5 mm) increments for safe processing. Each recipe in this book specifies the correct amount of headspace to use.

Jar lifter

If you buy only one canning gadget beyond the basics, a jar lifter (also known as canning tongs) is the one to get. With heatproof handles at one end and contoured, rubberized grabbers at the other for gripping jars under the neck, this tool will help you safely and securely move hot jars into and out of boiling water.

Kitchen scale

A small kitchen scale is an invaluable tool in the canning kitchen for best results and reliable yields. Packaging alone can't be relied upon for accurate weight measurements. For example, a 5-lb bag of apples usually weighs a little more than 5 lb. Weigh your ingredients at home on your own kitchen scale or use the scales available where you buy your ingredients. The right weights will lead to the best results.

Magnetic lid lifter

This pen-sized stick with a magnet attached at one end allows you to remove lids from hot water without burning your fingers or damaging the soft compound on the underside of the lid. It's an example of how simple tools can elevate your canning experience from finicky to fun.

Processing Checklist

Use this handy step-by-step processing checklist to safely preserve each recipe in this book. Simply prepare your chosen recipe, then follow these 10 easy steps.

1. Fill jars
Make sure your canning jars are spotlessly clean before using, and inspect them for chips and cracks that could lead to breakage or prevent a good seal. Sterilizing jars is not necessary for the recipes in this book (see page 4). If you will be filling your jars with hot preserves, keep them in hot water until just before filling to avoid sudden temperature changes that could crack the jars. For cold-packed preserves such as dill pickles, start with room-temperature jars. A ladle and canning funnel will help make filling jars quick and tidy.

2. Check headspace
Headspace is the gap between the top surface of the food and the rim of the jar. The correct amount of headspace ensures a strong vacuum seal as jars cool. Some foods, such as jams and jellies, expand less during processing than whole or sliced foods like tomatoes and peaches, so follow the recommended headspace for each recipe. Too much headspace could lead to a weak seal, and too little headspace could cause foods to spill out onto the jar rim during processing, also preventing a good seal. A headspace measuring tool will help you quickly and easily check for accuracy.

3. Remove air bubbles
If the recipe recommends removing air bubbles, poke a non-metallic utensil inside each jar a few times to release any pockets of air. Use a plastic knife, wooden chopstick, narrow rubber spatula or headspace measuring tool/bubble remover to do the job. Do not use a metal knife or spoon, which could crack hot jars.

After removing bubbles, check the headspace again and top up with more of the preserves if necessary to reach the recommended headspace.

4. Wipe jar rims

Use a clean, damp cloth or paper towel to remove any food spills from the jar rims before securing the lids. Bits of food or stickiness between the lid and the glass rim could prevent a seal during processing. It's also a good idea to wipe away food spills from around the jar threads where the screw bands come into contact with the glass.

5. Screw on lids

Follow the manufacturer's instructions on the packaging for preparing lids for processing. Position new flat lids over the clean jar rims and secure in place by twisting on the screw bands just until fingertip tight, which is just past the point of resistance. Not too tight—some air will need to escape during processing.

6. Lower jars into canner

It's a good idea to fill your canner with water and set it over high heat at least 20 minutes before you need it so it'll be boiling when the jars are ready to be processed. Larger canning pots may need longer for the water to come to a boil. If using a jar lifter, secure it under the neck of each filled jar to transfer it into the rack, keeping jars level to prevent food from spilling onto the jar rim. When the rack is lowered, make sure there is at least 1 inch (2.5 cm) of water above the jars. You may want to keep a kettle of boiling water handy in case you need to top up the water level once you lower your jars into the canner. Keep your canning pot covered with a lid when not moving jars in and out to maintain high heat and reduce evaporation.

7. Start timing

Wait until the water in the canner returns to a full boil before you start timing. Follow the recommended processing time for each recipe. Check the altitude chart (page 9) for timing adjustments if you live more than 1,000 feet (305 metres) above sea level. When the processing time is up, turn off the heat and remove the lid. Leave the jars in the canner for 5 more minutes.

8. Remove jars from canner

Granite, marble and other cool surfaces can crack hot jars, so line the kitchen counter with a kitchen towel if necessary. Remove the processed jars from the canner, keeping them level, and place them on the kitchen counter. Leave a little space between the jars for air circulation. Leave the jars on the counter to cool for 12 to 24 hours. Some jars will seal right away, making an obvious popping sound as they do. Others may take longer to seal. Do not tighten the screw bands while the jars are cooling.

9. Check seals

Once the jars are fully cooled, press the middle of each lid to check for a vacuum seal. If the centre of the lid is suctioned down, your jar has safely sealed. Occasionally, for various reasons, a lid won't seal and the centre will pop up and down when pressed. Simply store that jar in the fridge and consume it first. Screw bands are often loose after jars cool completely, which is perfectly normal.

10. Label and store

Label your jars with the contents and date. New jars often come with a sheet of sticker labels, but you can also write directly on the disposable lid with a permanent marker. Store canned foods in a cool, dark place and consume within 1 year. Screw bands can be left on or removed during storage. Opened jars must be refrigerated. Plastic mason jar storage lids are commonly available in standard and wide-mouth sizes and are useful to switch to once a jar is opened.

JAMS

Turning juicy fruit into sweet, jammy goodness is one of the most satisfying ways I spend time in the canning kitchen. A big pot of fruit bubbling away on the stove is about slowing down to indulge in the tastes, the smells and the beautiful colours of the season. Starting with fruit grown in my own garden is super-satisfying, but I also love a good chat with a local grower or greengrocer about what's available and what will be harvested soon. People who grow and sell produce are passionate about freshness and can offer helpful advice on how to choose the best-quality ingredients for your jam. I like to go in with a friend on buying a case of local berries, or get a whole case for my own kitchen and freeze half for making jam another day.

Everyone has their favourite jams. Mine are Apple Pie Jam (page 22), Sour Cherry Jam (page 41) and Red Plum Jam (page 37). I like to set aside a couple of hours for jam making so I can take plenty of time to put on some jazz, prepare the fruit slowly, snap a few photos of my yummy preserves along the way, then sit down with a cup of tea to admire my pretty jars as they cool.

But all those jewel-toned jams don't just belong on toast. There are plenty of other delicious ways to showcase your beautiful homemade jams. Top muffins and cheesecakes, fill blind-baked tart shells, add to icings for cakes and cupcakes, stir into oatmeal or plain yogurt, spoon onto pancakes and waffles, shake with vinegar and oil for a fruity vinaigrette, and even mix into a one-of-a-kind cocktail.

APPLE PIE JAM • STRAWBERRY JAM • STRAWBERRY RHUBARB JAM
RHUBARB JAM • BLACKBERRY VANILLA JAM • BLUEBERRY LIME JAM
TRIPLE BERRY JAM • RED PLUM JAM • SWEET CHERRY SUNRISE JAM
SOUR CHERRY JAM • KIWI JAM • GINGER PEAR JAM • APRICOT JAM
NECTARINE VANILLA BEAN JAM • PEACH JAM
RASPBERRY COCOA JAM • LEMON RASPBERRY JAMALADE

Apple Pie Jam

The classic taste of apple pie is just a jar away with this delicious jam made with tender diced apples and comforting cinnamon. Serve with freshly baked muffins and scones, spread on hot buttered toast or stir a spoonful into a bowl of oatmeal for a warm, cinnamon-scented breakfast. You'll want to grab a knife and start spreading pure apple pie joy on anything and everything.

MAKES SIX 250 ML (1 CUP) JARS
3 lb (1.4 kg) pie apples, such as Gala or Granny Smith
1 cup (250 mL) water
2 tbsp (30 mL) lemon juice
1½ tsp (7 mL) cinnamon
1 package (57 g) regular pectin powder
4 cups (1 L) granulated sugar
½ cup (125 mL) brown sugar

Remove and discard the apple peels and cores. Dice the apples, adding them to a large, heavy-bottomed pot. Pour in the water and lemon juice. Bring to a boil over high heat. Reduce the heat to medium-low and simmer, covered, for 10 to 15 minutes until the apples are soft.

Crush with a masher to a smoother but still chunky consistency. Stir in the cinnamon and pectin powder. Bring the works back up to a boil over high heat, stirring frequently. Stir in the granulated and brown sugars. Bring the works back up to a boil again over high heat. Maintain a hard boil for 1 minute. Remove the jam from the heat. Stir for 5 minutes to cool a little and prevent floating fruit.

Ladle into 6 clean 250 mL (1 cup) jars, leaving a ¼-inch (5 mm) headspace. Process in a boiling water bath canner for 15 minutes using the Processing Checklist on page 17.

TIP Use your favourite pie apple to make this jam. If you don't have a favourite, ask a friend who loves to make pie what variety they like best. My favourite is Gala for its complex pear-like flavour when cooked. You can use a mix of apples, too. Cinnamon is an apple-pie classic. For something different, try adding a little ground nutmeg, ginger, cloves or allspice to find the spice blend you like best.

Strawberry Jam

This jam reminds me of childhood and strawberry picking with my dad in rural Ontario. Strawberry jam is a canning classic and an ideal place to start for first-time jam makers. The process is simple and the results are spectacular. Begin with the best berries you can get your hands on, then enjoy your delicious jam on buttered toast and other bakery goodies. To turn a simple white cake into a strawberry cake, spread jam between the cake layers and stir some more strawberry jam into the icing.

MAKES SEVEN 250 ML (1 CUP) JARS
2½ lb (1.125 kg) strawberries
1 tbsp (15 mL) lemon juice
1 package (57 g) regular pectin powder
6 cups (1.5 L) granulated sugar

Rinse the strawberries under cool running water. Hull the berries, discarding the stems and leaves. Crush the berries with a masher in a large, heavy-bottomed pot (you should have about 4½ cups/1.125 L of crushed berries).

Stir in the lemon juice and pectin powder. Bring to a full boil over highest heat, stirring frequently. Pour in the sugar and return to a full rolling boil, stirring constantly. Maintain a hard foamy boil for 1 minute.

Remove from the heat. Skim off and discard the foamy pink scum. Stir your jam for a couple of minutes to allow it to cool just a little to prevent floating fruit.

Ladle into 7 clean 250 mL (1 cup) jars, leaving a ¼-inch (5 mm) headspace. Process in a boiling water bath canner for 15 minutes using the Processing Checklist on page 17.

TIP Unlike pickles and relishes, which get tastier in the jar over time, strawberry jam is best the day you make it. Rather than make a couple of batches the same day, I like to freeze strawberries when they're in season to make another batch a few months later.

STRAWBERRY RHUBARB JAM

Juicy strawberries and tart rhubarb go hand in hand and taste like sunny summer days in the garden. This jam is perfect for filling blind-baked tart shells and spooning over banana pancakes or waffles with whipped cream. Save a spot for a pretty jar of this jam in your picnic basket, right between the scones and the wine.

MAKES SEVEN 250 ML (1 CUP) JARS

1½ lb (675 g) strawberries
1 lb (450 g) rhubarb stalks
1 package (57 g) regular pectin powder
6 cups (1.5 L) granulated sugar

Rinse the strawberries under cool running water. Hull the berries, discarding the stems and leaves. Crush the strawberries with a masher in a large, heavy-bottomed pot (you should have about 2½ cups/625 mL of crushed berries).

Rinse the rhubarb under cool running water. Chop into ½-inch (1 cm) pieces and add them to the berries.

Stir in the pectin powder. Bring to a full boil over high heat, stirring frequently. Reduce the heat to medium and stir in the sugar. Once the sugar dissolves, increase the heat to high and bring the jam back to a hard boil. Maintain a full boil for 1 minute. Remove from the heat. Skim off and discard any foamy scum.

Ladle into 7 clean 250 mL (1 cup) jars, leaving a ¼-inch (5 mm) headspace. Process in a boiling water bath canner for 15 minutes using the Processing Checklist on page 17.

TIP Fresh garden strawberries and rhubarb can be chopped and frozen for making jam another day. Spread on a baking sheet and freeze before transferring to freezer bags or containers. Allow to thaw before making jam. You do not need to drain off any juices.

RHUBARB JAM

This sweet-meets-tart jam brings back memories of sitting on the front stoop of our house as a kid, dipping a stalk of freshly cut rhubarb into a small bowl of sugar on a hot day. Stir a few spoonfuls of this jam into some yogurt and freeze in moulds for creamy rhubarb yogurt pops. Making this perfectly pink jam during rhubarb season means daydreaming about hot and hazy summer days.

MAKES SIX 250 ML (1 CUP) JARS
1½ lb (675 g) rhubarb stalks
1½ cups (375 mL) water
1 package (57 g) regular pectin powder
6 cups (1.5 L) granulated sugar

Rinse the rhubarb under cool running water. Chop into ½-inch (1 cm) pieces. In a large, heavy-bottomed pot, bring the rhubarb and water to a boil over high heat. Reduce the heat to medium and cook, covered, for 5 minutes to soften.

Stir in the pectin powder. Cover and continue cooking for 2 more minutes. Stir in the sugar. Turn the heat back to high and bring the jam up to a full rolling boil, uncovered and stirring constantly. Maintain a hard foamy boil for 1 minute. Remove from the heat. Skim off and discard the foamy pink scum.

Ladle into 6 clean 250 mL (1 cup) jars, leaving a ¼-inch (5 mm) headspace. Process in a boiling water bath canner for 15 minutes using the Processing Checklist on page 17.

TIP Fresh rhubarb should feel firm and crisp. Store it in the fridge and use within a few days, or chop and store in the freezer for up to 6 months. The colour of your jam depends on the colour of your rhubarb. Young, red stalks make for a vibrant pink jam, but jam made with green rhubarb is just as tasty.

BLACKBERRY VANILLA JAM

This dark and sophisticated flavour combination is a jam lover's dream. Blackberries grow in abundance in my neighbourhood, and jam and pie are my favourite ways to make the most of their deep, juicy flavour. Dipping a spoon into a jar of luscious blackberries scented with delicate vanilla makes breakfast in bed an event. Add a spoonful to a breakfast smoothie or stir into plain yogurt for a yummy afternoon snack.

MAKES SEVEN 250 ML (1 CUP) JARS

3 lb (1.4 kg) blackberries
1 package (57 g) regular pectin powder
1 tbsp (15 mL) pure vanilla extract
5 cups (1.25 L) granulated sugar

Rinse the blackberries under cool running water. In a large, heavy-bottomed pot, crush the blackberries with a masher (you should have about 5 cups/1.25 L of crushed berries).

Stir in the pectin powder. Bring the mixture to a full rolling boil over highest heat, stirring frequently. Stir in the vanilla and sugar. Return to a full hard boil over highest heat. Maintain a full foamy boil for 1 minute. Remove from the heat. Skim off and discard any foamy scum.

Ladle into 7 clean 250 mL (1 cup) jars, leaving a ¼-inch (5 mm) headspace. Process in a boiling water bath canner for 15 minutes using the Processing Checklist on page 17.

TIP For best flavour, choose blackberries that are dark, plump and sweet. Picking berries yourself or as a group is a fun and inexpensive way to fill your jam jars with some of summer's best flavours.

Blueberry Lime Jam

This delightfully dark and delicious jam brings out the very best in blueberries. Start with plump, fresh berries and add a little zing of lime. I gave a jar of this to my son's teacher once and she was still raving about it months later. Blueberry fans will want to spread it on everything from English muffins to French toast—or just eat it straight from the jar with a spoon!

MAKES EIGHT 250 ML (1 CUP) JARS

3 lb (1.4 kg) blueberries
Zest and juice of 1 lime
1 package (57 g) regular pectin powder
5 cups (1.25 L) granulated sugar

Rinse the blueberries under cool running water, removing any stems. Drain well. In a large, heavy-bottomed pot, crush the blueberries with a masher to release their juices.

Stir in the lime zest, lime juice and pectin powder. Bring to a full boil over highest heat, stirring frequently. Stir in the sugar. Return to a full rolling boil, stirring constantly. Maintain a hard boil for 1 minute. Remove from the heat. Skim off and discard any foamy scum.

Ladle into 8 clean 250 mL (1 cup) jars, leaving a ¼-inch (5 mm) headspace. Process in a boiling water bath canner for 15 minutes using the Processing Checklist on page 17.

TIP Jars of jams like this one make a thoughtful gift for family and friends. Attach a personal message by tying a simple gift tag with twine under the ring band.

Triple Berry Jam

No need to choose just one type of juicy berry for your jam. This three-berry jam uses fresh raspberries, strawberries and blueberries for a very berry flavour that will please all the jam lovers in your life. Bake into jam squares or spread between shortbread cookie cut-outs for yummy snacks the kids will love.

MAKES SIX 250 ML (1 CUP) JARS
2 cups (500 mL) crushed raspberries (about 1 ½ lb/675 g raspberries)
1 ½ cups (375 mL) crushed strawberries (about 1 lb/450 g strawberries)
1 ½ cups (375 mL) whole blueberries
1 package (57 g) regular pectin powder
5 cups (1.25 L) granulated sugar

Combine the crushed raspberries, crushed strawberries and blueberries in a large, heavy-bottomed pot. Stir in the pectin powder. Bring the mixture to a full boil over high heat, stirring frequently. Stir in the sugar. Bring the jam back up to a full boil, stirring constantly to prevent scorching. Maintain a hard foamy boil for 1 minute. Remove from the heat. Skim off the foamy scum.

Ladle into 6 clean 250 mL (1 cup) jars, leaving a ¼-inch (5 mm) headspace. Process in a boiling water bath canner for 15 minutes using the Processing Checklist on page 17.

TIP Substitute blackberries for half of the raspberries for a Four Fieldberry Jam.

Red Plum Jam

Inexpensive plums make one of the tastiest jams on the breakfast table. While any plum variety can be jammed, red-fleshed plums in particular make for a show-stopping jam with a jewel-like colour and deep, juicy flavour. This one will always be on my pantry shelves for stirring into cool, creamy yogurt and spreading onto toast with peanut butter in the morning.

MAKES SEVEN 250 ML (1 CUP) JARS
3 lb (1.4 kg) red-fleshed plums
1 package (57 g) regular pectin powder
4 cups (1 L) granulated sugar

Rinse the plums under cool running water. Cut into chunks, leaving the skins on, and discarding the pits as you go. Crush the plums in a large, heavy-bottomed pot with a masher.

Stir in the pectin powder. Bring to a full boil over highest heat, stirring frequently. Stir in the sugar. Return to a full rolling boil, stirring constantly. Maintain a full foamy boil for 1 minute. Remove from the heat. Skim off and discard any foamy scum.

Ladle into 7 clean 250 mL (1 cup) jars, leaving a ¼-inch (5 mm) headspace. Process in a boiling water bath canner for 15 minutes using the Processing Checklist on page 17.

TIP Plum varieties come in different skin and flesh colours. Any red, black, yellow, purple or green plums can be used to make this jam. Have fun experimenting with different varieties or try a mixture of plums in the same batch.

Sweet Cherry Sunrise Jam

Cherry fans will fall hard for this fun and fruity loose-set jam. Dip a spoon into a jar and find bits of sweet cherries suspended in dark cherry-charged goodness. Use it to top a banana split or spoon over waffles and finish with cool whipped cream.

MAKES SEVEN 250 ML (1 CUP) JARS
3 lb (1.4 kg) dark sweet cherries
Zest and juice of 1 navel orange
1 package (57 g) regular pectin powder
6 cups (1.5 L) granulated sugar

Rinse the cherries under cool running water, removing any stems. Remove the pits and coarsely chop the cherries (you should have about 5 cups/1.25 L chopped cherries).

In a large, heavy-bottomed pot, stir together the cherries, orange zest and juice, and pectin powder. Bring to a full boil over high heat while stirring. Stir in the sugar. Return to a full hard boil over high heat, stirring constantly. Maintain a full foamy boil for 1 minute. Remove from the heat. Skim off and discard the foamy scum.

Ladle into 7 clean 250 mL (1 cup) jars, leaving a ¼-inch (5 mm) headspace. Process in a boiling water bath canner for 15 minutes using the Processing Checklist on page 17.

TIP Look for sweet cherries that are firm and shiny with attached stems. A cherry pitter is a very useful tool when processing a lot of cherries and can speed up your jam making.

SOUR CHERRY JAM

Sour cherries, also known as tart cherries, make the very best cherry pies and jams, and home cooks will go to great lengths to get their hands on them. Sour cherries have a very short season, so get them while you can to make this heavenly jam that will become one of your most prized preserves. Keep it simple and enjoy with a cup of tea on buttered toast, English muffins or scones.

MAKES FIVE 250 ML (1 CUP) JARS
2½ lb (1.125 kg) sour cherries
1 package (57 g) regular pectin powder
5 cups (1.25 L) granulated sugar

Rinse the cherries under cool running water. Pluck off the stems and remove the pits. Crush the cherries with a masher in a large, heavy-bottomed pot.

Stir in the pectin powder. Bring the cherries to a full rolling boil over high heat, stirring frequently. Stir in the sugar. Return to a full foamy boil over highest heat, stirring constantly. Maintain a hard boil for 1 minute. Remove from the heat. Skim off and discard the foamy scum. Stir the jam for a couple of minutes to allow it to cool just a little so the fruit won't float in your jars.

Ladle into 5 clean 250 mL (1 cup) jars, leaving a ¼-inch (5 mm) headspace. Process in a boiling water bath canner for 15 minutes using the Processing Checklist on page 17.

TIP Sour cherries are usually available fresh only in regions near where they're grown, or from specialty greengrocers. Store fresh sour cherries in the fridge and use within a few days.

KIWI JAM

This memorable jam is a standout for its bright flavour, glorious emerald colour and dramatic black seeds. Bring a jar out to share with special guests and treasured friends, and serve with slices of lemon loaf or flaky croissants from your favourite bakery and cups of green tea.

MAKES FIVE 250 ML (1 CUP) JARS

2½ lb (1.125 kg) kiwi fruit
1 package (57 g) regular pectin powder
5 cups (1.25 L) granulated sugar

Using a knife, peel the kiwi fruit, discarding the skins. Dice the fruit, adding the pieces to a large, heavy-bottomed pot. Crush with a masher if you want smaller pieces in your jam.

Stir in the pectin powder. Bring to a full boil over highest heat, stirring frequently. Stir in the sugar. Return to a full rolling boil, stirring constantly. Maintain a full boil for 1 minute. Remove from the heat. Skim off and discard any foamy scum.

Ladle into 5 clean 250 mL (1 cup) jars, leaving a ¼-inch (5 mm) headspace. Process in a boiling water bath canner for 15 minutes using the Processing Checklist on page 17.

TIP Size doesn't matter when it comes to kiwi fruit; large or small, they're equally delicious. Choose kiwis that are unblemished and firm but give slightly when pressed.

Ginger Pear Jam

Jam lovers will swoon for this striking flavour combination. Sweet, juicy pears and bright, zingy ginger make for a memorable jar of jam that also makes a lovely gift. At breakfast, add a spoonful to a banana smoothie or enjoy on warm carrot muffins. At dinner, make a quick vinaigrette by shaking a spoonful of jam in a jar with oil, vinegar and a pinch of salt, then pour over a pear and endive salad.

MAKES SIX 250 ML (1 CUP) JARS

2½ lb (1.125 kg) ripe pears
¼ cup (60 mL) finely chopped crystallized ginger
2 tbsp (30 mL) lemon juice
1 package (57 g) regular pectin powder
4½ cups (1.125 L) granulated sugar

Remove and discard the pear peels, stems and cores. Coarsely chop the pears, then crush them with a masher in a large heavy-bottomed pot.

Stir in the ginger, lemon juice and pectin powder. Bring to a full boil over highest heat, stirring frequently. Stir in the sugar. Return to a full foamy boil, stirring constantly. Maintain a full boil for 1 minute. Remove from the heat. Skim off and discard any foamy scum.

Ladle into 6 clean 250 mL (1 cup) jars, leaving a ¼-inch (5 mm) headspace. Process in a boiling water bath canner for 15 minutes using the Processing Checklist on page 17.

TIP Unlike most tree fruit, pears don't ripen on the tree. Instead, they're picked at maturity and kept in cold storage. To ripen pears at home, keep them at room temperature for 3 to 5 days until soft when gently pressed at the neck. Crystallized ginger, also called candied ginger, can be found in the baking aisle or bulk section of most grocery stores.

APRICOT JAM

With its bright flavour and colour, apricot jam is often a top pick of jam enthusiasts. This jam is simple to make, as the skins are left on and apricots are easy to pit and chop. Pick up some fresh apricots while they're in season, then enjoy them in this jam all the year through. Try this one baked into oat squares or thumbprint cookies, or whisk together with ketchup, vinegar and a little chili oil for a quick chicken grilling sauce.

MAKES SEVEN 250 ML (1 CUP) JARS
3 lb (1.4 kg) ripe apricots
2 tbsp (30 mL) lemon juice
1 package (57 g) regular pectin powder
5 cups (1.25 L) granulated sugar

Rinse the apricots under cool running water. Finely chop the apricots, leaving the skins on, discarding the pits as you go.

In a large, heavy-bottomed pot, combine the apricots and lemon juice. Stir in the pectin powder. Bring to a boil over high heat, stirring constantly. Lower the heat to medium. Pour in the sugar and continue stirring until the sugar is fully dissolved. Return the heat to high and bring the jam up to a full boil. Maintain a full foamy boil for 1 minute. Remove from the heat.

Ladle into 7 clean 250 mL (1 cup) jars, leaving a ¼-inch (5 mm) headspace. Process in a boiling water bath canner for 15 minutes using the Processing Checklist on page 17.

TIP Choose unblemished apricots that give slightly when gently squeezed. Apricots can be less juicy than other jam fruits, so it's important to keep stirring after the sugar is added to prevent scorching. It may be helpful to have your sugar measured and set aside before you begin cooking.

NECTARINE VANILLA BEAN JAM

One of my favourite fruits to eat fresh, succulent nectarines also make a beautiful jam. Here they're combined with classic and comforting vanilla seeds for an extra-special spread. Enjoy on toast or spoon over slices of cheesecake or scoops of ice cream.

MAKES FIVE 250 ML (1 CUP) JARS

2½ lb (1.125 kg) nectarines
1 vanilla bean
1 package (57 g) regular pectin powder
5 cups (1.25 L) granulated sugar

Using a sharp knife, score an X in the bottom of each nectarine. Plunge them whole into a large pot of boiling water for 1 minute, then transfer with a slotted spoon to a large bowl of cold water. Slip off and discard the skins. Holding each nectarine over a large, heavy-bottomed pot, tear open the fruit, discarding the pits. (If using clingstone nectarines, simply cut out the pits with a knife.) Use a masher to crush the fruit into a chunky consistency.

Using a small sharp knife, slice the vanilla bean in half lengthwise. Using the back of the knife, scrape out the tiny black vanilla seeds. Add them to the pot, along with the bean itself.

Stir in the pectin powder. Bring the mixture to a full boil, stirring constantly to prevent scorching. Stir in the sugar. Return to a boil, stirring constantly. Maintain a full foamy boil for 1 minute. Remove from the heat. Skim off any foamy scum and discard the vanilla bean.

Ladle into 5 clean 250 mL (1 cup) jars, leaving a ¼-inch (5 mm) headspace. Process in a boiling water bath canner for 15 minutes using the Processing Checklist on page 17.

TIP A pink/orange blush varies depending on the variety of nectarine, but isn't an indicator of ripeness. Instead, choose nectarines with a vivid yellow background colour. If your nectarines are firm when purchased, leave them at room temperature for a few days to become ripe, juicy and tender to the touch.

Peach Jam

Enjoy the flavour of drip-down-your-chin peaches any time of year with this delectable jam. Pull out a jar at breakfast to spread on hot buttered toast or muffins, or stir into plain yogurt for a peachy breakfast or snack. In the evening, a spoonful of this jam shaken with peach schnapps, orange juice and ice makes for a delicious cocktail garnished with a sprig of fresh rosemary.

MAKES SIX 250 ML (1 CUP) JARS
2½ lb (1.125 kg) peaches
1 package (57 g) regular pectin powder
5 cups (1.25 L) granulated sugar

With a sharp knife, score an X in the bottom of each peach. Plunge them whole into a large pot of boiling water for 1 minute, then transfer with a slotted spoon to a large bowl of cold water. Slip off and discard the skins. Pull or cut out the pits. Finely chop the peaches or crush with a masher in a large, heavy-bottomed pot.

Stir in the pectin powder. Bring to a full boil over high heat, stirring frequently. Stir in the sugar. Return to a full foamy boil over highest heat, stirring constantly. Maintain a hard boil for 1 minute. Remove from the heat. Skim off and discard the foamy scum. Stir the jam for a couple of minutes to lower the temperature just a bit to prevent floating fruit.

Ladle into 6 clean 250 mL (1 cup) jars, leaving a ¼-inch (5 mm) headspace. Process in a boiling water bath canner for 15 minutes using the Processing Checklist on page 17.

TIP To ensure ripeness before you get started, bite into each peach to make sure it's juicy, sweet and fresh enough to go into your homemade jam. Both clingstone and freestone peaches can be used for making jam, although freestone are a little easier to prepare because the pits aren't attached to the flesh.

RASPBERRY COCOA JAM

Classic raspberry jam gets a sinful twist with pure cocoa powder. Share spooned onto brownies and topped with whipped cream and chocolate shavings for a special dessert with someone you love, or whisk with a little dessert wine in a small saucepan until warm and pour over chocolate gateau. You've never had a jam like this before.

MAKES SEVEN 250 ML (1 CUP) JARS
2½ lb (1.125 kg) raspberries
1 tbsp (15 mL) lemon juice
¼ cup (60 mL) pure cocoa powder
1 package (57 g) regular pectin powder
6 cups (1.5 L) granulated sugar

Rinse the raspberries under cool running water and drain well. Crush the berries in a large, heavy-bottomed pot with a masher (you should have just about 5 cups/1.25 L of crushed berries).

Stir in the lemon juice, cocoa powder and pectin powder. Bring to a full boil over high heat, stirring frequently. Stir in the sugar. Return to a full boil, stirring constantly. Maintain a full boil for 1 minute. Remove from the heat. Skim off and discard any foamy scum.

Ladle into 7 clean 250 mL (1 cup) jars, leaving a ¼-inch (5 mm) headspace. Process in a boiling water bath canner for 15 minutes using the Processing Checklist on page 17.

TIP Milk products aren't safe for water bath canning, so it's important to use a pure cocoa powder that has no added milk solids. Look for one that lists only cocoa powder in the ingredients.

LEMON RASPBERRY JAMALADE

Jam meets marmalade in this fun and fruity spread that uses fresh raspberries as well as freshly squeezed lemon juice and thinly sliced lemon peel. Enjoy your own afternoon tea by spreading this on freshly baked scones and topping with traditional clotted cream. Pinkies up!

MAKES SIX 250 ML (1 CUP) JARS

2 lb (900 g) raspberries
1 lb (450 g) lemons
1 package (57 g) regular pectin powder
5½ cups (1.375 L) granulated sugar

Rinse the raspberries under cool running water and drain well. In a large, heavy-bottomed pot, crush the berries well with a masher.

Scrub the lemons under cool running water. Slice the lemons in half and juice thoroughly into the pot, skimming off and discarding the seeds. Using a metal spoon, scrape out and discard the membranes from the lemon halves, then slice off and discard the stem and blossom ends. Slice the peels very thinly, adding them to the pot with the raspberries.

Bring the works to a boil over high heat. Maintain a full boil for 2 to 3 minutes, stirring frequently. Stir in the pectin powder and keep boiling for another minute. Stir in the sugar and return to a full foamy boil, stirring constantly. Maintain a full foamy boil for 1 minute. Remove from the heat.

Ladle into 6 clean 250 mL (1 cup) jars, leaving a ¼-inch (5 mm) headspace. Process in a boiling water bath canner for 15 minutes using the Processing Checklist on page 17.

TIP Raspberries are very tender and can deteriorate quickly if not properly stored. Keep fresh raspberries in the fridge, and don't rinse them until you're ready to use them. Fresh berries can be frozen for making preserves another day. Simply spread them out on a baking sheet in the freezer, then transfer the frozen berries to freezer bags and store for up to 6 months. This method keeps the berries separated so you can take out just what you need for a batch of jam.

JELLIES AND MARMALADES

Jellies are some of the most beautiful and versatile preserves in any canning kitchen. Unlike jams, which are made with crushed or chopped fruit, most jellies are made with the juice strained from cooked fruit. The result is a colourful, transparent preserve that catches the morning sun beautifully at the breakfast table. Each time I make a new batch of jelly I leave some jars on my kitchen window ledge for a few days so I can enjoy their cheery colour. Jellies are a fun canvas on which to add a variety of other flavours such as garlic, fresh herbs and hot peppers. My absolute favourite is Garlic Rosemary Apple Jelly (page 62), which I often bring along to potluck parties as part of a cheese and crackers platter. Pepper jellies such as Hellfire Orange Habanero Jelly (page 66) are also absolutely lovely with soft cheeses or used as a glaze for roasted meats.

Marmalades, and some jellies, will form a gel set using the naturally occurring pectin found in citrus, apples and some other fruits. Wonderfully old-fashioned, marmalade is a preserve that people love to be persnickety about. Thick cut or paper thin, whole fruit or just the juice, oranges or other citrus (try my favourite, Coconut Lime Marmalade, on page 93), opinions abound on what makes the very best marmalade. Whether you go for the classic or the contemporary, it all makes for interesting breakfast conversation.

CORONATION GRAPE JELLY • TART GREEN APPLE JELLY
GARLIC ROSEMARY APPLE JELLY • RED PEPPER JELLY
HELLFIRE ORANGE HABANERO JELLY • PINEAPPLE PEPPER JELLY
MANGO JALAPEÑO PEPPER JELLY • STRAWBERRY BALSAMIC JELLY
CURRANT JELLY • POMEGRANATE JELLY • MINT JELLY
PINK LEMONADE JELLY • THICK-CUT ORANGE MARMALADE
BLOOD ORANGE VANILLA MARMALADE • MANDARIN GINGER MARMALADE
MEYER LEMON MARMALADE • APRICOT LEMON MARMALADE
COCONUT LIME MARMALADE • BLUEBERRY ORANGE MARMALADE
PINEAPPLE ORANGE MARMALADE • RUBY RED HOT MARMALADE

Coronation Grape Jelly

Grape jelly is a kid classic that some of us never outgrew. Crown roasted meats with a glaze of grape jelly or slide a spoon into a jar of richly coloured grape goodness to make the best peanut butter and jelly sandwich you've ever had.

MAKES SIX 250 ML (1 CUP) JARS
3 lb (1.4 kg) Coronation or Concord grapes
1½ cups (375 mL) water
1 package (57 g) regular pectin powder
4½ cups (1.125 L) granulated sugar

Pluck the grapes from their stems and rinse under cool running water. Crush the grapes well with a masher in a large, heavy-bottomed pot. Pour in the water and bring to a boil over high heat. Reduce the heat to medium, cover, and continue cooking for 10 minutes.

Scoop the hot grape mixture into a jelly bag (or a colander lined with a double layer of dampened cheesecloth) suspended over a large bowl. Let it drip until you have 4 cups (1 L) of juice. (This can take a few hours.)

Pour the juice back into the rinsed pot. Stir in the pectin powder. Bring to a rolling boil over highest heat, stirring frequently. Stir in the sugar. Return to a full boil, stirring constantly. Maintain a full foamy boil for 1 minute. Remove from the heat. Skim off and discard any foamy scum.

Ladle into 6 clean 250 mL (1 cup) jars, leaving a ¼-inch (5 mm) headspace. Process in a boiling water bath canner for 15 minutes using the Processing Checklist on page 17.

TIP Canning traditionalists say you shouldn't squeeze the jelly bag. But if after a few hours you're just short of enough juice, go ahead and give the jelly bag a gentle squeeze.

Tart Green Apple Jelly

Tangy and sweet, this classic jelly gets its sunny, cheerful flavour from tart green apples and freshly squeezed lemon juice. Use it to add a touch of bright flavour to crackers and cheese or roasted meats, or simply spread generously onto fresh bread.

MAKES FIVE 250 ML (1 CUP) JARS

5 lb (2.25 kg) tart green apples, such as Granny Smith
7 cups (1.75 L) water
½ cup (125 mL) lemon juice
5 cups (1.25 L) granulated sugar

Rinse the apples under cool running water. Cut into quarters, including the pectin-rich skins, cores and seeds, and place in a large, heavy-bottomed pot. Pour in the water. Bring to a boil over high heat. Reduce the heat to medium and simmer, covered, for 10 minutes.

Crush the softened apples with a masher. Pop the lid back on and simmer for another 10 minutes.

Scoop the pulp into 2 jelly bags (or a colander lined with a double layer of dampened cheesecloth) suspended over a large bowl. Let it drip until you have 5½ cups (1.375 L) of juice, about 2 hours.

In the rinsed pot, combine the apple juice, lemon juice and sugar. Bring to a hard boil over highest heat. Maintain a full foamy boil, stirring frequently, until it reaches the gel stage, about 10 minutes (see "How to Test a Gel Set" on page 7). Remove from the heat. Skim off any foamy scum.

Ladle into 5 clean 250 mL (1 cup) jars, leaving a ¼-inch (5 mm) headspace. Process in a boiling water bath canner for 15 minutes using the Processing Checklist on page 17.

TIP This recipe can also be made with other tart apple varieties such as Winesap, Northern Spy and Gravenstein. Try apples with red skins for a pretty pink apple jelly.

GARLIC ROSEMARY APPLE JELLY

A jar of this dramatic jelly adds a special touch to a cheese and crackers platter or charcuterie board. It starts out as a classic apple jelly, but the addition of vinegar, minced garlic and fresh rosemary takes things over the top. Try pairing it with a smoked Cheddar, cured meats and marinated olives with crackers.

MAKES THREE 250 ML (1 CUP) JARS

3½ lb (1.6 kg) apples (any variety)
5 cups (1.25 L) water
3½ cups (875 mL) granulated sugar
⅔ cup (150 mL) white vinegar
2 tbsp (30 mL) chopped fresh rosemary
1 tbsp (15 mL) minced garlic

Rinse the apples under cool running water. Chop into chunks, including the pectin-rich skins, cores and seeds, and place in a large, heavy-bottomed pot. Pour in the water. Bring to a boil over high heat. Reduce the heat to medium, cover, and continue cooking for 30 minutes, until mushy, stirring occasionally.

Scoop the hot apple mixture into a jelly bag (or a colander lined with a double layer of dampened cheesecloth) suspended over a large bowl. Let it drip until you have 3½ cups (875 mL) of juice. (This can take a few hours.)

Pour the juice into the rinsed pot. Stir in the sugar, vinegar, rosemary and garlic. Bring to a full boil over highest heat. Maintain a full foamy boil, stirring frequently, until it reaches the gel stage, about 10 minutes (see "How to Test a Gel Set" on page 7). Remove from the heat and skim off any foamy scum.

Ladle into 3 clean 250 mL (1 cup) jars, leaving a ¼-inch (5 mm) headspace. Process in a boiling water bath canner for 15 minutes using the Processing Checklist on page 17.

TIP Use the freshest rosemary and garlic you can find. Your finished jelly is as good as the ingredients you lovingly add to it.

Red Pepper Jelly

This classic pepper jelly is beloved for its sweet and sour combination, ruby-red colour and just a hint of heat. I like to give jars of this jelly as gifts because almost everyone likes it. Try it spread onto a buttered bagel, or serve as a party appetizer with warm crostini and a soft cheese like Brie.

MAKES SIX 250 ML (1 CUP) JARS

1½ lb (675 g) red bell peppers (about 4 large peppers)
2 cups (500 mL) cider vinegar, divided
2 tsp (10 mL) dried chili flakes
1 package (57 g) regular pectin powder
5 cups (1.25 L) granulated sugar

Rinse the peppers under cool running water. Coarsely chop the peppers, discarding the seeds and stems. Place the peppers in a blender along with 1 cup (250 mL) of the vinegar. Purée until smooth.

Pour the purée into a large, heavy-bottomed pot. Stir in the chili flakes. Bring to a boil over high heat. Reduce the heat to medium and simmer, uncovered, for 5 minutes.

Stir in the pectin powder and remaining 1 cup (250 mL) of vinegar. Return to a full boil over highest heat. Stir in the sugar and return to a boil again, stirring frequently. Maintain a full boil for 2 minutes while stirring. Remove from the heat.

Ladle into 6 clean 250 mL (1 cup) jars, leaving a ¼-inch (5 mm) headspace. Process in a boiling water bath canner for 15 minutes using the Processing Checklist on page 17.

TIP Choose deeply red peppers for the brightest red jelly. For other jelly colours, try using orange or yellow bell peppers instead. If you like it a little hotter, include a couple of jalapeño peppers or even bird's-eye chilies in your pepper purée.

Hellfire Orange Habanero Jelly

Hot pepper fans will love turning up the heat with this fruity jelly made with ultra-hot habanero peppers and freshly squeezed orange juice. Try it brushed over grilled chicken legs, or enjoy with spreadable cheeses for a creamy, sweet, tangy and spicy combination you won't be able to get enough of.

MAKES SIX 250 ML (1 CUP) JARS

4 habanero peppers
3 cups (750 mL) freshly squeezed orange juice (about 6 large navel oranges)
2 cups (500 mL) cider vinegar
2 tsp (10 mL) dried chili flakes
1 package (57 g) regular pectin powder
5 cups (1.25 L) granulated sugar

Remove the stems from the habanero peppers and discard. Drop the whole peppers into a blender. Pour in the orange juice. Purée until the peppers are in tiny pieces.

Pour the purée into a large, heavy-bottomed pot. Stir in the vinegar, chili flakes and pectin. Bring to a full boil over highest heat. Stir in the sugar. Return to a full boil. Maintain a full foamy boil, stirring frequently, until it reaches the gel stage, which should take about 3 to 4 minutes (see "How to Test a Gel Set" on page 7). Remove from the heat.

Ladle into 6 clean 250 mL (1 cup) jars, leaving a ¼-inch (5 mm) headspace. Process in a boiling water bath canner for 15 minutes using the Processing Checklist on page 17.

TIP Habanero peppers are very hot—about 35 times hotter than jalapeño peppers. This method of puréeing the habaneros whole in the blender, rather than chopping them with a knife, lets you avoid getting the fiery juices on your hands.

PINEAPPLE PEPPER JELLY

Sweet and sizzling hot, this fantastic jelly is a jewel on my canning shelves. Try it with roasted pork or serve with soft cheeses and plantain chips for a tropical potluck platter like no other. Gilligan would have loved this jelly.

MAKES FIVE 250 ML (1 CUP) JARS

4 cups (1 L) diced fresh pineapple (about 1 pineapple)
2 cups (500 mL) cider vinegar, divided
4 bird's-eye chilies, including seeds, thinly sliced
1 tbsp (15 mL) dried chili flakes
2 packages (57 g each) regular pectin powder
4 cups (1 L) granulated sugar

Combine the diced pineapple and 1 cup (250 mL) of the vinegar in a blender. Purée until smooth.

Pour the purée into a large, heavy-bottomed pot. Add the bird's-eye chilies, chili flakes and remaining 1 cup (250 mL) of vinegar. Stir in both packages of pectin powder. Bring to a full rolling boil over highest heat, stirring frequently. Stir in the sugar. Bring it back up to a full rolling boil, stirring constantly. Maintain a full rolling boil for 1 minute. Remove from the heat.

Ladle into 5 clean 250 mL (1 cup) jars, leaving a ¼-inch (5 mm) headspace. Process in a boiling water bath canner for 15 minutes using the Processing Checklist on page 17.

TIP The colour of a pineapple's skin doesn't tell us much about its ripeness. Instead, choose one that is plump and firm, with green, fresh-looking leaves. To dice a pineapple, trim off the top and bottom, then stand the pineapple upright and slice downward to remove the skin in strips, taking care to remove all of the eyes. Slice the pineapple crosswise into rounds and dice, taking care not to use the firm core, as it is a little bitter compared to the sweet fruit surrounding it.

Mango Jalapeño Pepper Jelly

Fall in love with the tropical flavours in this jelly made with juicy mangoes and zingy jalapeño peppers. Try it with grilled fish or coconut prawn skewers for a warm taste of the tropics. I adore the look of this jelly as much as its sweet and spicy flavour.

MAKES SIX 250 ML (1 CUP) JARS

3 cups (750 mL) diced mango (about 2 large mangoes)
2 cups (500 mL) cider vinegar, divided
½ cup (125 mL) minced jalapeño peppers
1 package (57 g) regular pectin powder
5 cups (1.25 L) granulated sugar

Combine the diced mango and 1 cup (250 mL) of the vinegar in a blender. Purée until smooth.

Pour the purée into a large, heavy-bottomed pot. Stir in the remaining 1 cup (250 mL) of vinegar, minced jalapeño and pectin powder. Bring to a full rolling boil over highest heat, stirring frequently. Stir in the sugar. Bring the works back up to a full hard boil, stirring constantly. Maintain a full hard boil for 1 minute. Remove from the heat. Skim off and discard any foamy scum.

Ladle into 6 clean 250 mL (1 cup) jars, leaving a ¼-inch (5 mm) headspace. Process in a boiling water bath canner for 15 minutes using the Processing Checklist on page 17.

TIP Colour isn't a good indicator of a mango's ripeness. Instead, choose mangoes with wrinkle-free skins that give a little when pressed. Unripe mangoes can be kept at room temperature for a few days to ripen. Once soft and juicy, refrigerate until you're ready to use them.

Strawberry Balsamic Jelly

Few things complement sweet, juicy strawberries like complex balsamic vinegar. This dark and delicious jelly uses the whole strawberry instead of just the juice and goes with everything from a simple cheese tray to pâté to slow-cooked meats. Once friends try some, they'll be wanting to get their hands on their very own jar.

MAKES SIX 250 ML (1 CUP) JARS

2 lb (900 g) strawberries
1 cup (250 mL) balsamic vinegar
1 package (57 g) regular pectin powder
5 cups (1.25 L) granulated sugar

Rinse the strawberries under cool running water. Hull the berries, discarding the stems and leaves. Add the berries and balsamic vinegar to a blender and purée until smooth.

Pour the purée into a large, heavy-bottomed pot. Stir in the pectin. Bring to a boil over highest heat, stirring frequently. Stir in the sugar. Bring back up to a full rolling boil, stirring constantly. Maintain a hard boil for 1 minute. Remove from the heat. Skim off and discard any scum.

Ladle into 6 clean 250 mL (1 cup) jars, leaving a ¼-inch (5 mm) headspace. Process in a boiling water bath canner for 15 minutes using the Processing Checklist on page 17.

TIP Balsamic vinegars vary in flavour and quality. Choose your favourite, but be sure not to use one labelled "balsamic glaze," which has a thicker consistency and stronger flavour.

Currant Jelly

Deeply flavoured currants are rich in natural pectin, which makes them ideal for making jelly. Use black, red or white currants to make this jewel-like tasty treat. Enjoy on scones and muffins, or whisk a spoonful with a splash of wine to make a quick pan sauce for pork chops.

MAKES FIVE 250 ML (1 CUP) JARS
10 cups (2.5 L) fresh currants (any colour)
1 cup (250 mL) water
4½ cups (1.125 L) granulated sugar

Pluck the currants from their stems, if you prefer, or leave them in strigs, and rinse under cool running water. In a large, heavy-bottomed pot, crush the currants with a masher to release the juices. Pour in the water. Bring to a boil over high heat. Reduce the heat to medium, cover, and continue cooking for 10 minutes, stirring occasionally.

Scoop the hot pulp and liquid into a jelly bag (or a colander lined with a double layer of dampened cheesecloth) suspended over a large bowl. Let it drip until you have 3¼ cups (810 mL) of juice, which could take up to 2 hours. Gently squeeze the jelly bag to top up if you don't have enough juice.

Pour the juice into the rinsed pot. Stir in the sugar. Bring to a boil over highest heat, stirring constantly. Maintain a full boil, stirring frequently, until it reaches the gel stage, which should only take 1 to 2 minutes (see "How to Test a Gel Set" on page 7). Remove from the heat. Skim off and discard the scum.

Ladle into 5 clean 250 mL (1 cup) jars, leaving a ¼-inch headspace. Process in a boiling water bath canner using the Processing Checklist on page 17.

TIP To keep them fresh, currants are plucked in groupings called strigs. Measure your currants on their strigs and pluck only if you feel up to the tedious task. Otherwise, boil as they are.

POMEGRANATE JELLY

Wonderfully tart and sweet, this jelly makes a special treat for pomegranate fans. Shake with oil and vinegar for a quick and pretty vinaigrette, or try it as a special accompaniment for roasted turkey sandwiches instead of the traditional cranberry sauce.

MAKES FOUR 250 ML (1 CUP) JARS
6 large pomegranates
1 package (57 g) regular pectin powder
4 cups (1 L) granulated sugar

Score the pomegranates horizontally all the way around. Twist and pull apart. Holding one half at a time over a large, heavy-bottomed pot, hit the backs firmly with a heavy metal spoon to release the seeds (it may help to gently squeeze the pomegranate halves as you go). Remove and discard any pieces of the bitter white membrane from the pot.

Bring the seeds to a boil over high heat. Reduce the heat to medium and boil, covered, for 5 minutes to release the juice from the seeds.

Scoop the liquid into a jelly bag (or a colander lined with a double layer of dampened cheesecloth) suspended over a large bowl. Let it drip until you have 3 cups (750 mL) of strained juice, which could take up to 2 hours. Gently squeeze the jelly bag if necessary to get enough juice.

Pour the juice into the rinsed pot. Stir in the pectin powder. Bring to a full boil over highest heat, stirring frequently. Add the sugar and return to a full boil, continuing to stir frequently. Maintain a full foamy boil for 1 minute. Remove from the heat. Skim off and discard any foamy scum.

Ladle into 4 clean 250 mL (1 cup) jars, leaving a ¼-inch (5 mm) headspace. Process in a boiling water bath canner for 15 minutes using the Processing Checklist on page 17.

TIP Choose heavy pomegranates that are brightly coloured and shiny without blemishes. A pomegranate that is heavy means it has lots of juice inside, ideal for making jelly.

Mint Jelly

This is a canning classic and one of the most popular herb jellies. Try it the traditional way, served with roast lamb, or stir a spoonful into hot herbal tea to sweeten and add a touch of minty flavour at the same time.

MAKES FOUR 250 ML (1 CUP) JARS

2 cups (500 mL) gently packed fresh mint leaves
2½ cups (625 mL) water
2 tbsp (30 mL) lime juice
A few drops of green food colouring (optional)
1 package (57 g) regular pectin powder
4 cups (1 L) granulated sugar

Add the mint leaves and water to a medium saucepan. Bring just to a boil over high heat, then remove from the heat, cover, and set aside to allow the mint leaves to infuse the water for 20 minutes.

Strain the liquid into a large, heavy-bottomed pot, discarding the mint leaves. Stir in the lime juice, food colouring (if using) and pectin powder. Bring to a boil over highest heat. Stir in the sugar and return to a full foamy boil, stirring frequently. Maintain a hard boil for 1 minute. Remove from the heat. Skim off and discard the foamy scum.

Ladle into 4 clean 250 mL (1 cup) jars, leaving a ¼-inch (5 mm) headspace. Process in a boiling water bath canner for 15 minutes using the Processing Checklist on page 17.

TIP I prefer spearmint leaves, but peppermint and chocolate mint varieties also make lovely jelly. Mint comes back year after year in the garden and requires little care.

Pink Lemonade Jelly

This refreshing jelly tastes like summertime in a jar. Tart lemons and sweet, juicy strawberries combine for a distinctive jelly that makes a perfect pick-me-up with a morning or mid-afternoon pastry. This jelly is also a kid-favourite on nut butter sandwiches.

MAKES FOUR 250 ML (1 CUP) JARS

3 lb (1.4 kg) lemons
1 cup (250 mL) crushed strawberries (about ⅔ lb/300 g strawberries)
5 cups (1.25 L) water
3 cups (750 mL) granulated sugar

Scrub the lemons under cool running water. Slice the lemons in half crosswise, then cut each half into quarters. Add the lemon pieces to a large, heavy-bottomed pot along with the crushed strawberries and water. Bring to a boil over high heat. Reduce the heat to medium and simmer, uncovered and stirring occasionally, for 30 minutes to soften the lemons and release their natural pectin and juices.

Scoop the mixture into a jelly bag (or a colander lined with a double layer of dampened cheesecloth) suspended over a large bowl. Let it drip until you have 3½ cups (875 mL) of juice. (This could take up to an hour.)

Pour the juice into the rinsed pot. Stir in the sugar. Bring the mixture to a boil over highest heat, stirring constantly. Maintain a full foamy boil until it reaches the gel stage, about 2 minutes (see "How to Test a Gel Set" on page 7). Remove from the heat.

Ladle into 4 clean 250 mL (1 cup) jars, leaving a ¼-inch (5 mm) headspace. Process in a boiling water bath canner for 15 minutes using the Processing Checklist on page 17.

TIP The skins and seeds of lemons contain a lot of natural pectin, so there's no need to use additional pectin in this recipe. For a twist, substitute 1 cup (250 mL) of crushed raspberries, blackberries or blueberries for the strawberries and see what kind of jelly colours you can come up with.

THICK-CUT ORANGE MARMALADE

Using the freshly squeezed juice and sliced peel of oranges, this is marmalade the way it has been enjoyed for generations—thick cut and well set. Spread on hot buttered toast or English muffins for a sunny start to even the greyest of days.

MAKES SIX 250 ML (1 CUP) JARS
3 lb (1.4 kg) oranges
1 lemon
5 cups (1.25 L) water
6 cups (1.5 L) granulated sugar

Scrub the oranges and lemon under cool running water. Slice the fruit in half crosswise and juice thoroughly, pouring the juice into a large, heavy-bottomed pot and reserving the seeds and lemon halves in a medium bowl. Using a metal spoon, scrape out the membranes from the orange halves and add to the seeds. Slice off the stem and blossom ends and add to the seeds. Slice the orange peels up to ⅛-inch (3 mm) thick until you have 2½ cups (625 mL).

Add the sliced orange peel and water to the pot. Place the reserved seeds, lemon halves, orange membranes, stem and blossom ends and any remaining peel on a double-layer square of cheesecloth. Bring up the edges and tie with kitchen string to form a secure pouch. Nestle the pouch into the pot. Bring the works to a bubble over high heat. Reduce the heat to medium-low and simmer, covered, for 1 hour.

Scoop the pouch into a fine-mesh sieve and press on it with the back of a spoon to release the pectin-rich juices back into the pot. Discard the pouch. Stir in the sugar. Bring to a hard boil over highest heat, uncovered and stirring frequently. Maintain a full boil, still stirring, until it reaches the gel stage, which should take about 10 minutes (see "How to Test a Gel Set" on page 7). Remove from the heat.

Ladle into 6 clean 250 mL (1 cup) jars, leaving a ¼-inch (5 mm) headspace. Process in a boiling water bath canner for 15 minutes using the Processing Checklist on page 17.

TIP Commonly available navel orange varieties make perfectly delicious marmalade. For a bit of drama, try sweet Cara Cara navel oranges, Valencia oranges or sour Sevilles for a classic Dundee marmalade.

Blood Orange Vanilla Marmalade

Deeply coloured with the garnet-hued juice of blood oranges and dramatically scented with pure vanilla, this marmalade uses not just the juice and peel of the orange but the flesh. This one was made for breakfast in bed with flaky croissants and hot coffee.

MAKES SEVEN 250 ML (1 CUP) JARS
3 lb (1.4 kg) blood oranges
6 cups (1.5 L) water
6 cups (1.5 L) granulated sugar
2 tbsp (30 mL) pure vanilla extract

Scrub the oranges under cool running water. Slice off and discard the stem and blossom ends. Stand each orange upright and slice downward to remove the zest in strips, trying to remove just the coloured part, leaving most of the white pith behind. Slice the zest into very thin strips until you have 2½ cups (625 mL).

Cut away and discard the pith from the oranges. Slice the oranges in half crosswise and pick out and discard the seeds. Chop the flesh into small pieces.

In a large, heavy-bottomed pot, combine the sliced zest, chopped flesh and water. Bring the works to a boil over high heat. Reduce the heat to medium-low and simmer, covered, for 1 hour.

Stir in the sugar. Bring to a full boil over highest heat, uncovered and stirring constantly. Maintain a full boil, stirring frequently, until it reaches the gel stage, which should take about 15 to 20 minutes (see "How to Test a Gel Set" on page 7). Remove from the heat. Stir in the vanilla.

Ladle into 7 clean 250 mL (1 cup) jars, leaving a ¼-inch (5 mm) headspace. Process in a boiling water bath canner for 15 minutes using the Processing Checklist on page 17.

TIP Blood oranges have a delicious raspberry-like citrus flavour. Look for them in the winter months when they're in season.

Mandarin Ginger Marmalade

Naturally sweet and tender mandarins make a delicately delicious marmalade. Add a little lemon and ginger and the result is a refreshing twist on a classic. Try it with morning glory muffins for breakfast or a snack, or whisked with rice vinegar for a quick chicken stir-fry sauce.

MAKES SIX 250 ML (1 CUP) JARS
3 lb (1.4 kg) mandarin oranges (about 10 medium mandarins)
2 lemons
7 cups (1.75 L) water
6 cups (1.5 L) granulated sugar
1 tbsp (15 mL) grated fresh ginger

Scrub the mandarins and lemons under cool running water. Slice the fruit in half crosswise and juice thoroughly, pouring the juice into a large, heavy-bottomed pot and reserving the seeds in a medium bowl. Using a metal spoon, gently scrape out the membranes from the mandarin halves and add to the seeds. Slice off the stem and blossom ends and add to the seeds. Slice the mandarin peels into very thin strips until you have 2½ cups (625 mL).

Add the sliced mandarin peel and water to the pot. Place the reserved seeds, lemon halves, mandarin membranes, stem and blossom ends and any remaining peel on a double-layer square of cheesecloth. Bring up the edges and tie with kitchen string to form a secure pouch. Nestle the pouch into the pot. Bring to a boil over high heat. Reduce the heat to medium-low and simmer, covered, for 1 hour.

Scoop the pouch into a fine-mesh sieve and press on it with the back of a spoon to release the pectin-rich juices back into the pot. Discard the pouch. Stir in the sugar. Bring to a full foamy boil over highest heat and boil, stirring frequently, for 20 minutes. Stir in the ginger and continue boiling, stirring frequently, until it reaches the gel stage, which should take about 5 more minutes (see "How to Test a Gel Set" on page 7). Remove from the heat.

Ladle into 6 clean 250 mL (1 cup) jars, leaving a ¼-inch (5 mm) headspace. Process in a boiling water bath canner for 15 minutes using the Processing Checklist on page 17.

TIP Any sweet oranges labelled clementine, satsuma or tangerine will work nicely in this recipe. To get the most juice out of your oranges, use a manual or electric citrus reamer.

MEYER LEMON MARMALADE

Fragrant Meyer lemons have smooth, thin skins and are sweeter than common supermarket lemons, bringing a delicate floral note to this cheery marmalade. Spread a spoonful on a toasted English muffin or stir into hot tea for a comforting citrus warm-up.

MAKES FOUR 250 ML (1 CUP) JARS

2 lb (900 g) Meyer lemons
6 cups (1.5 L) water
4 cups (1 L) granulated sugar

Scrub the lemons under cool running water. Slice in half crosswise and juice thoroughly, pouring the juice into a large, heavy-bottomed pot and reserving the seeds in a medium bowl. Using a metal spoon, scrape out the membranes from the lemon halves and add to the seeds. Slice off the stem and blossom ends and add to the seeds. Slice all the peels into very thin strips.

Add the sliced peel and water to the pot. Place the reserved seeds, membranes, and stem and blossom ends on a double-layer square of cheesecloth. Bring up the edges and tie with kitchen string to form a secure pouch. Nestle the pouch into the pot. Bring to a boil over high heat. Reduce the heat to medium-low and simmer, covered, for 1 hour.

Scoop the pouch into a fine-mesh sieve and press on it with the back of a spoon to release the pectin-rich juices back into the pot. Discard the pouch. Stir in the sugar. Bring to a hard boil over highest heat and boil, stirring constantly, until it reaches the gel stage, which should take about 15 minutes (see "How to Test a Gel Set" on page 7). Remove from the heat.

Ladle into 4 clean 250 mL (1 cup) jars, leaving a ¼-inch (5 mm) headspace. Process in a boiling water bath canner for 15 minutes using the Processing Checklist on page 17.

TIP Look for Meyer lemons that have shiny, bright yellow skins and are heavy for their size. Layering two at a time on the cutting board will make slicing the peels quicker.

Apricot Lemon Marmalade

Anything made with apricots is an instant hit in my home, including this beautiful marmalade made with the juice and thinly sliced peel of lemons. For snacks and desserts, try it baked into oat squares or classic thumbprint cookies.

MAKES SEVEN 250 ML (1 CUP) JARS
2½ lb (1.125 kg) lemons
6 cups (1.5 L) water
2 cups (500 mL) finely diced apricots (unpeeled)
6 cups (1.5 L) granulated sugar

Scrub the lemons under cool running water. Cut in half crosswise and juice thoroughly, pouring the juice into a large, heavy-bottomed pot and saving the seeds in a medium bowl. Using a metal spoon, scrape out the membranes from about half of the lemon halves and add to the seeds. Slice off the stem and blossom ends of those halves and add to the seeds. Slice those peels into very thin strips until you have 2 cups (500 mL).

Add the sliced peel and water to the pot. Place the reserved seeds, membranes, stem and blossom ends and the remaining lemon halves on a double-layer square of cheesecloth. Bring up the edges and tie with kitchen string to form a secure pouch. Snuggle the pouch into the pot. Bring the works to a boil over high heat. Reduce the heat to medium-low and simmer, covered, for 1 hour.

Scoop the pouch into a fine-mesh sieve and press on it with the back of a spoon to release the pectin-rich juices back into the pot. Discard the pouch. Stir in the apricots and sugar. Bring to a full boil over highest heat, stirring frequently. Maintain a full foamy boil, stirring constantly, until it reaches the gel stage, which should take about 15 minutes (see "How to Test a Gel Set" on page 7). Remove from the heat.

Ladle into 7 clean 250 mL (1 cup) jars, leaving a ¼-inch (5 mm) headspace. Process in a boiling water bath canner for 15 minutes using the Processing Checklist on page 17.

TIP Apricots have an all-too-short season, and canning while they're available lets you indulge in their special flavour any time. You might even ask your local farm stand or greengrocer if a case price is available and make several apricot recipes at once.

COCONUT LIME MARMALADE

Start the day with the fun pairing of coconut and lime in this tropical twist that even marmalade traditionalists will love. Enjoy on a toasted English muffin or buttered bagel or as a glaze for grilled chicken. This one is so good, you'll want friends to have a jar too.

MAKES NINE 250 ML (1 CUP) JARS
3 lb (1.4 kg) limes
8 cups (2 L) water
6 cups (1.5 L) granulated sugar
1 cup (250 mL) sweetened shredded or flaked coconut

Scrub the limes under cool running water. Cut in half crosswise and juice thoroughly, pouring the juice into a large, heavy-bottomed pot. Using a metal spoon, scrape out the membranes and reserve in a small bowl. Slice off the stem and blossom ends and add them to the membranes. Slice the peels into very thin strips until you have 2 cups (500 mL).

Add the sliced peel and water to the pot. Place the reserved membranes, stem and blossom ends and any remaining peel on a double-layer square of cheesecloth. Bring up the edges and tie with kitchen string to form a secure pouch. Nestle the pouch into the pot. Bring the works to a boil over high heat. Reduce the heat to medium-low and simmer, covered, for 90 minutes.

Scoop the pouch into a fine-mesh sieve and press on it with the back of a spoon to release the pectin-rich juices back into the pot. Discard the pouch. Stir in the sugar and coconut. Bring to a full foamy boil over highest heat, stirring frequently. Maintain a full boil, still stirring frequently, until it reaches the gel stage, which should take about 10 minutes (see "How to Test a Gel Set" on page 7). Remove from the heat. Stir the marmalade for a couple of minutes, letting it cool just a little to prevent floating coconut.

Ladle into 9 clean 250 mL (1 cup) jars, leaving a ¼-inch (5 mm) headspace. Process in a boiling water bath canner for 15 minutes using the Processing Checklist on page 17.

TIP Ripe limes should be shiny and firm but not overly hard. Choose limes with the fewest blemishes, since you'll be using the peels in your marmalade.

Blueberry Orange Marmalade

Oranges and deeply coloured blueberries make for a fun and fruity marmalade that's as delicious as it is beautiful. Spread on homemade blueberry muffins or hot raisin toast for breakfast or a snack. This one makes a lovely gift, but you'll want to tuck away a few jars just for yourself.

MAKES SIX 250 ML (1 CUP) JARS
3 lb (1.4 kg) navel oranges (any variety)
6 cups (1.5 L) water
2 cups (500 mL) blueberries
6 cups (1.5 L) sugar

Scrub the oranges under cool running water. Slice in half crosswise and juice thoroughly, pouring the juice into a large, heavy-bottomed pot and saving the seeds in a medium bowl. Using a metal spoon, scrape out the membranes from the orange halves and add to the seeds. Trim off the stem and blossom ends and add to the seeds. Slice the peels into very thin strips until you have 2½ cups (625 mL).

Add the sliced peel and water to the pot. Place the saved seeds, membranes, stem and blossom ends and any remaining peel on a double-layer square of cheesecloth. Bring up the edges and tie with kitchen string to form a secure pouch. Nestle the pouch into the pot. Bring to a boil over high heat. Reduce the heat to medium-low and simmer, covered, for 30 minutes.

Scoop the pouch into a fine-mesh sieve and press on it with the back of a spoon to release the pectin-rich juices back into the pot. Discard the pouch. Stir in the blueberries and sugar. Bring to a full foamy boil over highest heat, stirring frequently. Maintain a boil, still stirring frequently, until it reaches the gel stage, which should take about 20 to 25 minutes (see "How to Test a Gel Set" on page 7). Remove from the heat.

Ladle into 6 clean 250 mL (1 cup) jars, leaving a ¼-inch (5 mm) headspace. Process in a boiling water bath canner for 15 minutes using the Processing Checklist on page 17.

TIP Look for plump, firm blueberries with a silvery sheen on the skins. Remove any stems and discard berries with broken skins. Blueberries freeze well, so it can be worth it to buy a large box when they're in season and freeze for making jams, jellies and marmalades another day.

Pineapple Orange Marmalade

Tender bits of sweet and juicy pineapple are right at home in the marmalade jar. Add a tropical touch to toast and scones, or try a few spoonfuls of this sunny spread with a slice of rum-soaked pound cake for a sassy pineapple pick-me-up.

MAKES SIX 250 ML (1 CUP) JARS

2½ lb (1.125 kg) navel oranges
2½ cups (625 mL) finely diced fresh pineapple (about half a pineapple)
6 cups (1.5 L) water
6 cups (1.5 L) granulated sugar

Scrub the oranges under cool running water. Slice in half crosswise and juice thoroughly, pouring the juice into a large, heavy-bottomed pot and saving the seeds in a medium bowl. Using a metal spoon, scrape out the membranes from the orange halves and add to the seeds. Slice off the stem and blossom ends and add to the seeds. Slice the peels into very thin strips until you have 2½ cups (625 mL).

Add the sliced peel, pineapple and water to the pot. Place the saved seeds, membranes, stem and blossom ends and any remaining peel on a double-layer square of cheesecloth. Bring up the edges and tie with kitchen string to form a secure pouch. Nestle the pouch into the pot. Bring to a boil over high heat. Reduce the heat to medium-low and simmer, covered, for 1 hour.

Scoop the pouch into a fine-mesh sieve and press on it with the back of a spoon to release the pectin-rich juices back into the pot. Discard the pouch. Stir in the sugar. Bring to a foamy boil over highest heat, stirring frequently. Maintain a full boil, still stirring frequently, until it reaches the gel stage, which should take about 20 to 25 minutes (see "How to Test a Gel Set" on page 7). Remove from the heat.

Ladle into 6 clean 250 mL (1 cup) jars, leaving a ¼-inch (5 mm) headspace. Process in a boiling water bath canner for 15 minutes using the Processing Checklist on page 17.

TIP Pineapple holds its shape when cooked, so whatever size you dice your pineapple is the size it will be in your finished marmalade.

Ruby Red Hot Marmalade

This sweet-with-heat marmalade will tickle your sweet tooth and wake up your taste buds at the same time. Try it with aged cheese on toasted pumpernickel or mix with a little rice vinegar and brush over juicy grilled chicken breasts.

MAKES SEVEN 250 ML (1 CUP) JARS

3 lb (1.4 kg) Ruby Red grapefruit (or any red or pink variety)
7 cups (1.75 L) water
4 bird's-eye chilies, thinly sliced
6 cups (1.5 L) granulated sugar

Scrub the grapefruit under cool running water. Slice in half crosswise and juice thoroughly, pouring the juice into a large, heavy-bottomed pot and reserving the seeds in a medium bowl. Using a metal spoon, scrape out the membranes from the grapefruit halves and add to the seeds. Slice off the stem and blossom ends and add to the seeds. Slice the peels into very thin strips until you have 2 cups (500 mL).

Add the sliced peel and water to the pot. Place the reserved seeds, membranes, stem and blossom ends and any remaining peel on a double-layer square of cheesecloth. Bring up the edges and tie with kitchen string to form a secure pouch. Nestle the pouch in the pot. Bring the works to a boil over high heat. Reduce the heat to medium-low and simmer, covered, for 90 minutes.

Scoop the pouch into a fine-mesh sieve and press on it with the back of a spoon to release the pectin-rich juices back into the pot. Discard the pouch. Stir in the chilies (including the seeds) and sugar. Bring to a full foamy boil over highest heat, stirring frequently. Maintain a full boil, still stirring frequently, until it reaches the gel stage, which should take about 15 minutes (see "How to Test a Gel Set" on page 7). Remove from the heat.

Ladle into 7 clean 250 mL (1 cup) jars, leaving a ¼-inch (5 mm) headspace. Process in a boiling water bath canner for 15 minutes using the Processing Checklist on page 17.

TIP Ruby Reds are sometimes labelled Texas Red, Rio Red or Rio Star. They all make very tasty marmalade. The perfect grapefruit should be heavy (an indicator of juiciness) and look like it's about to burst through its skin. Want it scorching hot? Try using a little habanero or Scotch bonnet pepper in your marmalade. Want it less spicy? Choose a jalapeño, or leave the pepper out altogether for a straightforward grapefruit marmalade.

PICKLES AND RELISHES

Pickles are about memories, childhood and traditions that comfort us. We might not remember exactly what went into grandma's dill pickles, but we remember how they made us feel. Every bite, every new jar opened, brings us back to grandma's table and fills us with the satisfaction that we can carry on the tradition of pickling in our own canning kitchen. Some of my favourite pickles are made with the humblest vegetables, such as beets and beans in a simple brine. My kids never seem to get enough of homemade Crunchy Dill Pickles (page 105)—we go through about 40 jars a year!

Relishes are sometimes thought of as a canning category of their own, but they are really chopped pickle mixtures. Relish has a long history in home canning as a way to safely preserve chopped vegetables like cucumbers, zucchini and peppers by adding acidic vinegar. The satisfyingly sour result works as a jumping-off point for a spectrum of other flavours such as spicy, smoky and sweet. Largely used as a condiment, relish is also one of the handiest preserves to use in home cooking. Add a few spoonfuls of any relish to picnic salads like potato or pasta salad, spoon corn relish onto tacos or fish, add zing to pasta dishes with a little tomato relish, and mix sweet green relish with mayonnaise for a quick tartar sauce for fish that's better than anything you'll find in stores. Relish is the friend of any dish that could use a little brightening.

Some recipes in this chapter call for pickling vinegar, which is 7% acetic acid and stronger than distilled white vinegar. Large jugs of pickling vinegar can often be found wherever canning supplies are sold. For all other pickling recipes, be sure to use vinegars that are at least 5% acetic acid for safe preserving.

Use pickling salt where it is called for in these recipes. Unlike table salt, coarse pickling salt is pure and doesn't contain iodine or anti-caking agents that could cloud your brine. Pickling salt is sometimes labelled canning salt or preserving salt. If you can't find pickling salt, pure sea salt or pure kosher salt are good alternatives.

BREAD AND BUTTER PICKLES • CRUNCHY DILL PICKLES
DOUBLE DILLY BEANS • HOT-AND-SOUR PICKLED GREEN BEANS
PICKLED SLICED BEETS • PICKLED ASPARAGUS SPEARS
TRIPLE RED PICKLE • PICKLED PEARL ONIONS • HOT PICKLED PEPPERS
SWEET GREEN RELISH • DILL PICKLE RELISH • HOT DOG RELISH
ZUCCHINI SWEET RELISH • TOMATO RED ONION RELISH
CHIPOTLE CHERRY TOMATO RELISH • RAINBOW PEPPER RELISH
SOUTHWEST CORN RELISH • FENNEL THYME RELISH

Bread and Butter Pickles

A classic in any canning kitchen, these bread and butter pickles make for a sweet-and-sour treat on the side of a sandwich plate or tucked under a burger bun.

MAKES SIX 500 ML (2 CUP) JARS

6 lb (2.7 kg) pickling or English cucumbers
2 cups (500 mL) thinly sliced white onion
⅓ cup (75 mL) pickling salt
2 cups (500 mL) pickling vinegar (7% acetic acid)
2 cups (500 mL) water
1½ cups (375 mL) granulated sugar
1 tbsp (15 mL) whole allspice
1 tbsp (15 mL) mustard seeds
1½ tsp (7 mL) celery seeds
½ tsp (2 mL) turmeric

Scrub the cucumbers under cool running water. Slice the cucumbers ¼ inch (5 mm) thick, discarding the tips as you go. Toss the cucumbers and onions with the salt in a very large bowl or pot. Let stand for 3 hours to allow the salt to draw excess moisture from the vegetables.

Drain the veggies and rinse well. In a large, heavy-bottomed pot, combine the vinegar, water, sugar, allspice, mustard seeds, celery seeds and turmeric. Bring to a boil over high heat. Add the veggies to the hot liquid and return to a boil. Remove from the heat.

Using a slotted spoon, scoop the pickles into 6 clean 500 mL (2 cup) jars. Top up with the pickling liquid, leaving a ½-inch (1 cm) headspace. Poke a non-metallic utensil inside each jar a few times to remove any air bubbles, topping up with the pickling liquid if necessary. Process in a boiling water bath canner for 10 minutes using the Processing Checklist on page 17.

TIP Whereas pickling cucumbers are usually available only mid to late summer, seedless English cucumbers are available year-round and make a great choice for bread and butter pickles. Try adding or substituting other spices in your pickling liquid, such as 1 tsp (5 mL) of whole cloves or coriander seeds. For best flavour, wait 2 to 3 weeks before opening.

CRUNCHY DILL PICKLES

The irresistible dill pickle is a canning classic and a fun project for first-time canners. Preserve them sliced for sandwiches and burgers, cut into spears for the side of your plate, or left whole for scrumptious hand-held snacks straight from the pickle jar. My kids love these so much, I make about 40 jars a year to get us through until next pickling-cucumber season.

MAKES EIGHT 500 ML (2 CUP) JARS
5 lb (2.25 kg) pickling cucumbers
16 garlic cloves, peeled
I large bunch of fresh dill
4 cups (I L) water
2¾ cups (675 mL) pickling vinegar (7% acetic acid)
⅓ cup (75 mL) pickling salt

Scrub the cucumbers well under cool running water. Line up 8 clean 500 mL (2 cup) jars. Drop 2 garlic cloves and a few large dill fronds into each jar. For whole pickles, pack the cucumbers snugly into the jars, starting with the larger ones and filling in gaps with smaller ones. (Cucumbers shrink a little during processing, so pack tightly.) For spears, cut into quarters lengthwise, then press back together before packing into jars to maintain crispness. For slices, slice lengthwise and hold together for packing into jars to maintain crispness.

Prepare the brine by combining the water, vinegar and salt in a large saucepan. Set over high heat and bring to a light boil, stirring while the salt dissolves and the liquid turns from cloudy to clear.

Ladle the hot brine over the packed cucumbers, leaving a ½-inch (1 cm) headspace. Process in a boiling water bath canner for 10 minutes using the Processing Checklist on page 17.

TIP For the crunchiest pickles, start with cucumbers that are firm and crisp, not rubbery, and plan to pickle them the day you buy or pick them. Avoid over-processing your jars. Have your canner at a rapid boil before lowering your jars into the water, and start timing as soon as the water returns to a boil. Experiment with adding some pickling spices to each jar such as dill seed, whole coriander seed, whole allspice or peppercorns. For best flavour, wait 3 to 4 weeks before opening.

Double Dilly Beans

These pretty pickled beans are packed with dill flavour, not just from fresh dill fronds but from flavourful dill seeds as well. Slip a few inside your burger bun, chop into salads, or just snack on them cold and crisp straight from the jar.

MAKES SIX 500 ML (2 CUP) JARS

4½ lb (2 kg) fresh green beans
6 garlic cloves, peeled
6 tsp (30 mL) dill seeds
I bunch of fresh dill
3 cups (750 mL) pickling vinegar (7% acetic acid)
3 cups (750 mL) water
¼ cup (60 mL) pickling salt

Rinse the beans under cool running water. Trim off and discard the tips at both ends. Line up 6 clean 500 mL (2 cup) jars. Drop 1 garlic clove, 1 tsp (5 mL) dill seeds and a few dill fronds into each jar. Pack the jars snugly with the beans, ensuring they come no higher than ¾ inch (2 cm) from the jar rim.

Make the brine by combining the vinegar, water and salt in a medium saucepan. Turn the heat to high and stir until the liquid goes from cloudy to clear and the salt is completely dissolved.

Ladle the brine over the beans, leaving a ½-inch (1 cm) headspace. Poke a non-metallic utensil inside each jar a few times to remove any air bubbles, topping up the brine if needed. Process in a boiling water bath canner for 10 minutes using the Processing Checklist on page 17.

TIP For the prettiest pickles, choose the freshest beans you can find. The quantity of beans in this recipe does account for some lesser quality beans to be discarded during preparation. To make packing the jars easier, start with the largest beans and fill in gaps with thinner beans. For best flavour, wait 2 to 3 weeks before opening.

Hot-and-Sour Pickled Green Beans

Personalize your Caesar or Bloody Mary cocktail by sliding one of these spicy and tangy pickled green beans into the glass. They're also fantastic chopped in salads and added to pasta dishes and omelettes. This is a simple canning project, ideal for first-time picklers.

MAKES FIVE 500 ML (2 CUP) JARS

3 lb (1.4 kg) green beans
2½ tsp (12 mL) dried chili flakes
5 garlic cloves, peeled
3 cups (750 mL) water
2¼ cups (550 mL) pickling vinegar (7% acetic acid)
¼ cup (60 mL) pickling salt

Rinse the beans under cool running water. Trim off and discard the tips at both ends. Line up 5 clean 500 mL (2 cup) jars. Put ½ tsp (2 mL) chili flakes and 1 garlic clove into each jar. Pack each jar with the green beans, ensuring they are at least ¾ inch (2 cm) below the jar rim.

Prepare the brine by combining the water, vinegar and salt in a large saucepan. Stir over high heat until the salt dissolves completely and the liquid turns from cloudy to clear.

Ladle the hot brine into the jars, leaving a ½-inch (1 cm) headspace. Poke a non-metallic utensil inside each jar a few times to remove any air bubbles, topping up the brine if necessary. Process in a boiling water bath canner for 15 minutes using the Processing Checklist on page 17.

TIP Quality fresh green beans should make a satisfying snap sound when broken. To simplify packing, use wide-mouth instead of standard-mouth canning jars. For even hotter flavour, add peppercorns or some brown mustard seeds to your jars. For best flavour, wait 2 to 3 weeks before opening.

PICKLED SLICED BEETS

With their rich purple colour and deep, earthy flavour, the pickled beet is the queen of all root vegetables. Pull out a jar of these magnificent beet slices to be the crowning jewel in your favourite salads.

MAKES FIVE 500 ML (2 CUP) JARS

4 lb (1.8 kg) beets
3 cups (750 mL) white vinegar
1 ½ cups (375 mL) water
3 tbsp (45 mL) pickling salt
2 tbsp (30 mL) granulated sugar

Boil the whole unpeeled beets in a large pot of water for 30 to 35 minutes or until fork-tender. Drain and set aside until cool enough to handle. Trim off and discard the root and stem ends. Slip off and discard the skins. Slice the beets ¼ inch (5 mm) thick. Layer the slices snugly into 5 clean 500 mL (2 cup) jars up to 1 inch (2.5 cm) from the jar rim.

Make the brine by combining the vinegar, water, salt and sugar in a large saucepan. Bring to a boil over high heat, stirring to fully dissolve the sugar and salt.

Ladle the hot brine over the packed beets, leaving a ½-inch (1 cm) head-space. Poke a non-metallic utensil inside each jar a few times to remove any air bubbles, topping up the brine if necessary. Process in a boiling water bath canner for 15 minutes using the Processing Checklist on page 17.

TIP Disposable food service gloves are useful when preparing beets to prevent purple-stained hands. Experiment with flavours by adding spices like peppercorns, slices of ginger or sprigs of rosemary to jars before filling with beets. For best flavour, wait 2 to 3 weeks before opening.

PICKLED ASPARAGUS SPEARS

These savoury spears of pickled asparagus are seasoned with flavourful fennel seeds and a garlic clove inside each jar. Enjoy a couple of spears alongside a deli sandwich, or chopped and tossed with your favourite hot or cold pasta dishes.

MAKES THREE 500 ML (2 CUP) JARS

4 lb (1.8 kg) asparagus
3 garlic cloves, peeled
1½ tsp (7 mL) fennel seeds
1¾ cups (425 mL) pickling vinegar (7% acetic vinegar)
1½ cups (375 mL) water
2 tbsp (30 mL) pickling salt

Rinse the asparagus under cool running water. Cut the spears into about 4-inch (10 cm) lengths. Line up 3 clean 500 mL (2 cup) jars. Drop 1 garlic clove and ½ tsp (2 mL) fennel seeds into each jar. Snugly pack the spears upright into the jars, ensuring they're at least ¾ inch (2 cm) below the rim.

Prepare the brine by combining the vinegar, water and salt in a medium saucepan. Stir over high heat until the salt dissolves and the liquid turns from cloudy to clear.

Ladle the hot brine over the packed asparagus, leaving a ½-inch (1 cm) headspace. Poke a non-metallic utensil inside each jar a few times to remove any air bubbles, topping up the brine if needed. Process in a boiling water bath canner for 10 minutes using the Processing Checklist on page 17.

TIP For crispy pickles, choose thick, firm asparagus stalks rather than thin ones. Simplify packing by using wide-mouth canning jars. For best flavour, wait 2 to 3 weeks before opening.

Triple Red Pickle

This red cabbage and red onion pickle in red wine vinegar is a lovely example of the simplicity and affordability of home canning. Scoop a forkful of this tasty pickle onto cheese toasties for a satisfying lunch or appetizer to share. Use a splash of the flavourful brine when making gravy from beef drippings.

MAKES FOUR 500 ML (2 CUP) JARS

2½ lb (1.125 kg) red cabbage (about 1 large head)
2 cups (500 mL) thinly sliced red onion
4 cups (1 L) red wine vinegar
¼ cup (60 mL) pickling salt
¼ cup (60 mL) granulated sugar
1 tbsp (15 mL) celery seeds

Peel off and discard the outside leaves of cabbage. Cut the cabbage in half. Cut out and discard the firm white core. Cut each half in half lengthwise, then slice thinly into crosswise strips, or slice (not shred) in a food processor.

In a large pot, combine the cabbage, red onion, vinegar, salt, sugar and celery seeds. Turn the heat to high and cook, stirring constantly, just until the liquid comes to a boil. Remove from the heat.

Using tongs or a slotted spoon, scoop the softened veggies into 4 clean 500 mL (2 cup) jars up to 1 inch (2.5 cm) from the rim. Top up with the vinegar cooking liquid, leaving a ½-inch (1 cm) headspace. Poke a non-metallic utensil inside each jar a few times to release any air bubbles, topping up the liquid if necessary. Process in a boiling water bath canner for 20 minutes using the Processing Checklist on page 17.

TIP Play around with spices to personalize your red pickle. Try adding whole allspice, fennel seeds, peppercorns or a few whole cloves per jar. For best flavour, wait 2 to 3 weeks before opening.

PICKLED PEARL ONIONS

The satisfying, one-bite appeal of a pickled pearl onion is hard to resist. Pearl onions are sweeter than common onions and come in gold, white and red varieties. Toss into salads or serve on a toothpick with a cocktail. On the side of a sandwich plate, they're a burst of homemade flavour that'll make you smile every time.

MAKES THREE 500 ML (2 CUP) JARS
3 lb (1.4 kg) gold, white or red pearl onions
2½ cups (625 mL) white vinegar
½ cup (125 mL) water
1 tbsp (15 mL) pickling salt

Drop the onions into a large pot of boiling water and boil for 3 minutes, then transfer immediately to a large bowl of cold water. Cut off and discard the root ends, then slip off the skins by gently squeezing the onions out through the root end. Fill 3 clean 500 mL (2 cup) jars with the peeled onions up to 1 inch (2.5 cm) from the rim.

Add the vinegar, water and salt to a large saucepan. Bring just to a boil over high heat, stirring to fully dissolve the salt.

Ladle the hot liquid over the onions, leaving a ½-inch (1 cm) headspace. Process in a boiling water bath canner for 15 minutes using the Processing Checklist on page 17.

TIP It takes about a pound of pearl onions to fill one 500 mL (2 cup) jar. With that 1:1 ratio in mind, this recipe can easily be doubled. For tangiest flavour, wait 2 weeks before opening.

HOT PICKLED PEPPERS

You'll want to add these zesty peppers to just about everything. Tuck a few inside a toasted sandwich or a burger, chop into sauces or make them your new favourite pizza topping. A little bit of zing is always a good thing!

MAKES FIVE 500 ML (2 CUP) JARS

4 lb (1.8 kg) fresh hot peppers (mostly banana peppers plus other narrow peppers for colour)
4 cups (1 L) pickling vinegar (7% acetic acid)
2 cups (500 mL) water
¼ cup (60 mL) pickling salt

Rinse the peppers under cool running water. Trim off and discard the stem ends. Pull out and discard the ribs. Give each pepper a shake or rinse again to dislodge most of the seeds. Slice the peppers into rings ⅛ inch (3 mm) thick.

In a large pot, bring the vinegar, water and salt to a boil. Add the pepper rings to the pot and return just to a boil. Remove from the heat.

Using a slotted spoon, scoop the peppers equally into 5 clean 500 mL (2 cup) jars. Ladle the hot cooking liquid over the peppers, leaving a ½-inch (1 cm) headspace. Poke a non-metallic utensil inside each jar a few times to remove any air bubbles, topping up the cooking liquid if needed. Process in a boiling water bath canner for 10 minutes using the Processing Checklist on page 17.

TIP Pale green banana peppers are mildly hot and turn yellow when pickled. Good choices to add to the mix are hot Fresno, poblano or Anaheim peppers. For a milder mix, choose sweet mini bell peppers. For best flavour, wait at least 2 weeks before opening.

Sweet Green Relish

Sweet and tangy cucumber relish is a canning classic. Use a spoonful on burgers and hot dogs or in egg salad and other sandwich mixtures, or stir some into mayonnaise for a quick, best-ever tartar sauce for fish and chips.

MAKES FOUR 500 ML (2 CUP) JARS

4 lb (1.8 kg) cucumbers
2½ cups (625 mL) finely diced yellow onion
¾ cup (175 mL) finely diced green bell pepper
½ cup (125 mL) finely diced red bell pepper
¼ cup (60 mL) pickling salt
2½ cups (625 mL) white vinegar
1¾ cups (425 mL) granulated sugar
1 tbsp (15 mL) celery seeds

Rinse the cucumbers under cool running water. Trim off and discard the tips. Finely dice the cucumbers (or coarsely shred using a box grater, or chop in a food processor). In a large bowl, stir together the cucumber, onion, green pepper, red pepper and salt. Let stand for 1 hour to allow the salt to draw excess moisture from the vegetables.

Drain and rinse the vegetables in a large fine-mesh sieve or a colander lined with a large double layer of cheesecloth. Firmly squeeze out the excess liquid. Transfer the vegetables to a large, heavy-bottomed pot. Stir in the vinegar, sugar and celery seeds. Bring to a boil over high heat. Reduce the heat to medium and continue cooking for 5 minutes, stirring frequently. Remove from the heat.

Ladle into 4 clean 500 mL (2 cup) jars, leaving a ½-inch (1 cm) headspace. Poke a non-metallic utensil inside each jar a few times to remove any air bubbles, topping up the relish if necessary. Process in a boiling water bath canner for 15 minutes using the Processing Checklist on page 17.

TIP Any cucumber variety can be used for making relish. The English cucumber is a good choice for its firmness, thin skin and nearly seedless interior.

DILL PICKLE RELISH

Get all the satisfying pucker of a crunchy dill pickle in this easy-to-make relish. Combine shredded cucumbers with chopped fresh dill and minced garlic, then pickle it all in a classic salt-and-vinegar brine. Kids and adults love this one on hamburgers and hot dogs and stirred into tuna salad or egg salad for sandwiches.

MAKES THREE 500 ML (2 CUP) JARS
10 cups (2.5 L) shredded or finely chopped cucumber
¼ cup (60 mL) pickling salt
6 garlic cloves, minced
½ cup (125 mL) finely chopped fresh dill
2½ cups (625 mL) white vinegar
2 tbsp (30 mL) granulated sugar

In a large bowl, stir together the cucumber and salt. Set aside for 1 hour to allow the salt to draw excess moisture from the cucumber.

Drain and rinse the cucumber in a large fine-mesh sieve or a colander lined with a large double layer of cheesecloth. Firmly squeeze out the excess liquid. Transfer the cucumber to a large, heavy-bottomed pot. Stir in the garlic, dill, vinegar and sugar. Bring to a boil over high heat. Reduce the heat to medium and continue cooking for 5 minutes, stirring frequently. Remove from the heat.

Ladle into 3 clean 500 mL (2 cup) jars, leaving a ½-inch (1 cm) headspace. Poke a non-metallic utensil inside each jar a few times to remove any air bubbles, topping up the relish if necessary. Process in a boiling water bath canner for 15 minutes using the Processing Checklist on page 17.

TIP You can use pickling cucumbers to make this relish or any other firm cucumber such as commonly available English cucumbers. One English cucumber will give you about 3 cups (750 mL) shredded or finely chopped.

Hot Dog Relish

Half mustard, half relish, this tangy condiment takes burgers and dogs to the next level. Keep a jar handy during grilling season, as this one will become a quick favourite. Try it on smokies and bratwurst too.

MAKES THREE 500 ML (2 CUP) JARS

4 lb (1.8 kg) cucumbers
2 cups (500 mL) finely diced yellow onion
½ cup (125 mL) finely diced red bell pepper
¼ cup (60 mL) pickling salt
2½ cups (625 mL) white vinegar
1 cup (250 mL) granulated sugar
½ cup (125 mL) dry mustard
2 tbsp (30 mL) yellow mustard seeds
1 tbsp (15 mL) turmeric

Rinse the cucumbers under cool running water. Trim off and discard the tips. Coarsely shred the cucumbers using a box grater or finely chop in a food processor. In a large bowl, stir together the cucumber, onion, red pepper and salt. Let stand for 1 hour to allow the salt to draw the excess moisture from the vegetables.

Drain and rinse the vegetables in a large fine-mesh sieve or a colander lined with a double layer of cheesecloth. Squeeze out the excess liquid. Transfer the vegetables to a large, heavy-bottomed pot. Stir in the vinegar, sugar, dry mustard, mustard seeds and turmeric. Bring to a boil over high heat. Reduce the heat to medium and continue cooking, stirring frequently, for 5 minutes. Remove from the heat.

Ladle into 3 clean 500 mL (2 cup) jars, leaving a ½-inch (1 cm) headspace. Poke a non-metallic utensil inside each jar a few times to release any air bubbles, topping up the relish if necessary. Process in a boiling water bath canner for 15 minutes using the Processing Checklist on page 17.

TIP Dry mustard is sometimes labelled ground mustard or mustard powder. It's all ground yellow mustard seeds, and it adds a tangy, satisfying zing to your cooking.

Zucchini Sweet Relish

This incredibly tasty relish is a perfect way to use up an abundance of fresh garden zucchini in summer. Use it on barbecue night with cheeseburgers and smokies or add a few spoonfuls to your meatloaf mixture. If there's a perfect relish, this is it.

MAKES FOUR 500 ML (2 CUP) JARS

3 lb (1.4 kg) zucchini
2½ cups (625 mL) finely diced yellow onion
1 cup (250 mL) finely diced red bell pepper
¾ cup (175 mL) finely diced green bell pepper
¼ cup (60 mL) pickling salt
2½ cups (625 mL) granulated sugar
2½ cups (625 mL) white vinegar
1 tbsp (15 mL) celery seeds
1 tbsp (15 mL) yellow mustard seeds

Rinse the zucchini under cool running water. Trim off and discard the tips. Coarsely shred the zucchini on a box grater or finely chop in a food processor. In a large bowl, stir together the zucchini, onion, red pepper, green pepper and salt. Let stand for 1 hour to allow the salt to draw excess moisture from the vegetables.

Drain and rinse the vegetables in a fine-mesh sieve or a colander lined with a large double layer of cheesecloth. Firmly squeeze out the excess liquid. Transfer the vegetables to a large, heavy-bottomed pot. Stir in the sugar, vinegar, celery seeds and mustard seeds. Bring to a bubble over high heat. Reduce the heat to medium and continue cooking, stirring frequently, for 5 minutes. Remove from the heat.

Ladle into 4 clean 500 mL (2 cup) jars, leaving a ½-inch (1 cm) headspace. Poke a non-metallic utensil inside each jar a few times to remove any air bubbles, topping up the relish if necessary. Process in a boiling water bath canner for 15 minutes using the Processing Checklist on page 17.

TIP For a flavour twist, experiment with brown or black mustard seeds. The darker the mustard seed, the hotter they are. For a colour twist, try sunny yellow zucchini instead of green.

TIP The best relish starts with the best ingredients. Use the juiciest plump tomatoes you can find. For a spicy tomato relish, add some cayenne pepper along with the other spices.

Tomato Red Onion Relish

Enjoy your sun-ripened garden tomatoes all year in this classic hamburger relish that will bring back memories of barbecues gone by. A few spoonfuls of this tomato relish also brighten up pasta and rice dishes, or mix with sour cream to make a delicious chip dip.

MAKES FIVE 500 ML (2 CUP) JARS

7 lb (3.2 kg) tomatoes
4 cups (1 L) finely diced red onion
1½ cups (375 mL) finely diced red bell pepper
⅓ cup (75 mL) pickling salt
4 garlic cloves, crushed
3 cups (750 mL) red wine vinegar
¾ cup (175 mL) granulated sugar
2 tbsp (30 mL) celery seeds
1 tbsp (15 mL) mustard seeds
½ tsp (2 mL) ground allspice
¼ tsp (1 mL) ground cloves

Using a sharp knife, score an X in the bottom of each tomato. Immerse the tomatoes in a large pot of boiling water for 1 minute, then transfer with a slotted spoon to a large bowl of cold water. (You may prefer to do this in batches.) Slip off and discard the skins. Dice the tomatoes, adding them to a large colander lined with a double layer of cheesecloth. Add the onion and red pepper. Gently stir in the salt. Let drain for 1 hour, in the sink or over a large bowl, as the salt draws excess moisture from the vegetables.

Rinse the veggies under cool running water and drain well. Gather up the edges of the cheesecloth and squeeze out the excess water. Transfer the veggies to a large, heavy-bottomed pot. Stir in the garlic, vinegar, sugar, celery seeds, mustard seeds, allspice and cloves. Bring to a boil over high heat. Reduce the heat to medium-high and continue boiling, stirring frequently, for 10 minutes. Remove from the heat.

Ladle into 5 clean 500 mL (2 cup) jars, leaving a ½-inch (1 cm) headspace. Poke a non-metallic utensil inside each jar a few times to remove any air bubbles, topping up the relish if needed. Process in a boiling water bath canner for 20 minutes using the Processing Checklist on page 17.

CHIPOTLE CHERRY TOMATO RELISH

You've never had relish like this before. Halved cherry tomatoes are combined with finely chopped red peppers and onions, then seasoned with big spices like chipotle and cumin. I love this one at breakfast, spooned over scrambled eggs on toast. Smoky, sour, sweet and spicy, it's an instant favourite of anyone who loves relish—and maybe even those who don't.

MAKES FIVE 500 ML (2 CUP) JARS

3 lb (1.4 kg) cherry or grape tomatoes
2 lb (900 g) red onions
1 lb (450 g) red bell peppers
⅓ cup (75 mL) pickling salt
2¾ cups (675 mL) cider vinegar
1¼ cups (300 mL) granulated sugar
2 tsp (10 mL) chipotle chili powder
1 tsp (5 mL) celery seeds
½ tsp (2 mL) ground cumin

Rinse the tomatoes under cool running water. Slice in half, adding them to a colander lined with a large double layer of cheesecloth. Peel the red onions. Remove the stems, ribs and seeds from the red peppers. Using a knife or a food processor, finely chop the onions and peppers, then add them to the colander with the tomatoes. Gently stir in the salt. Let drain for 1 hour, in the sink or over a large bowl, as the salt draws excess moisture from the vegetables.

Rinse the veggies under cool running water. Gather up the edges of the cheesecloth and squeeze out the excess liquid. Transfer the mixture to a large, heavy-bottomed pot. Stir in the vinegar, sugar, chipotle, celery seeds and cumin. Bring to a boil over high heat, stirring frequently. Reduce the heat to medium and continue cooking, stirring frequently, for about 8 minutes, until the tomatoes are no longer firm. Remove from the heat.

Ladle into 5 clean 500 mL (2 cup) jars, leaving a ½-inch (1 cm) headspace. Poke a non-metallic utensil inside each jar a few times to release any air bubbles, topping up the relish if necessary. Process in a boiling water bath canner for 20 minutes using the Processing Checklist on page 17.

TIP To halve small tomatoes quickly, spread them in a single layer between two dinner plates, then run a long sharp knife between the plates. A chipotle is a smoked and dried mature jalapeño pepper. It's important to use powdered chipotle rather than chipotle peppers in oil because oils shouldn't be boiling water bath canned. Most grocery stores sell this popular spice in powdered form, and all spice merchants will carry it.

Rainbow Pepper Relish

Use a rainbow of bell peppers to make this tasty relish that goes great with burgers, grilled meats and vegetables and spread inside a grilled cheese sandwich. It turns out rainbows are as delicious as you thought they were.

MAKES FOUR 500 ML (2 CUP) JARS

5 lb (2.25 kg) bell peppers in various colours
1 lb (450 g) yellow onions
¼ cup (60 mL) pickling salt
3 cups (750 mL) cider vinegar
1½ cups (375 mL) granulated sugar
1 tbsp (15 mL) celery seeds
1 tbsp (15 mL) mustard seeds

Rinse the peppers under cool running water. Cut them in half and remove the stems, ribs and seeds. Finely chop the peppers using a knife or food processor. Peel the onions and finely chop using a knife or food processor. Add the peppers and onions to a large colander lined with a double layer of cheesecloth. Gently stir in the salt. Let drain for 1 hour in the sink or over a large bowl.

Rinse the vegetables under cool running water. Gather up the edges of the cheesecloth and press out the excess liquid. Transfer the vegetables to a large, heavy-bottomed pot. Stir in the vinegar, sugar, celery seeds and mustard seeds. Bring to a boil over high heat, stirring frequently. Lower the heat to medium and simmer for 5 minutes, stirring frequently. Remove from the heat.

Ladle into 4 clean 500 mL (2 cup) jars, leaving a ½-inch (1 cm) headspace. Poke a non-metallic utensil inside each jar a few times to remove any air bubbles, topping up the relish if necessary. Process in a boiling water bath canner for 15 minutes using the Processing Checklist on page 17.

TIP Bell peppers come in green, red, orange, yellow, white and even purple. Use a mixture of colours to get the look you want for your relish. Look for peppers that are firm with shiny, wrinkle-free skins and healthy-looking stems.

SOUTHWEST CORN RELISH

Add a little zing to grilled fish or tacos, or enjoy a heaping spoonful of this relish on a steaming bowl of chili. For a quick and tasty dip, mix your corn relish with some sour cream, then grab some tortilla chips and start dipping.

MAKES SIX 500 ML (2 CUP) JARS

10 cups (2.5 L) fresh or frozen corn kernels (see Tip for how to measure)
2½ cups (625 mL) finely diced yellow onion
2½ cups (625 mL) finely diced red bell pepper
1 cup (250 mL) finely diced green bell pepper
2 jalapeño peppers, finely diced
2 tbsp (30 mL) celery seeds
1 tbsp (15 mL) chili powder
2 tsp (10 mL) turmeric
4 cups (1 L) white vinegar
1 tbsp (15 mL) pickling salt
2 cups (500 mL) granulated sugar

Measure the corn and set aside. In a large, heavy-bottomed pot, combine the onion, red pepper, green pepper, jalapeños, celery seeds, chili powder, turmeric, vinegar and salt. Boil over high heat for 5 minutes. Stir in the sugar and corn. Return to a boil and cook for another 5 minutes at full heat, stirring frequently. Remove from the heat.

Ladle into 6 clean 500 mL (2 cup) jars, leaving a ½-inch (1 cm) headspace. Poke a non-metallic utensil inside each jar a few times to release any air bubbles, topping up the relish if necessary. Process in a boiling water bath canner for 15 minutes using the Processing Checklist on page 17.

TIP You'll need 14 to 16 medium cobs. Blanch first by boiling the husked cobs in water for 3 minutes, then transfer immediately to ice water. Slice off the kernels in strips into a large bowl. Break up the kernels by hand, then measure. Frozen corn measures differently than thawed. If using frozen sweet corn, thaw first by rinsing in a colander under warm running water, then measure.

Fennel Thyme Relish

Anise-flavoured fennel makes a distinctive and flavourful white relish. Try this thyme-flecked relish with your favourite grilled sausages or on a toasted corned beef sandwich for a twist on a classic Reuben.

MAKES FOUR 500 ML (2 CUP) JARS
4 fennel bulbs
2½ cups (625 mL) finely chopped yellow onion
3 tbsp (45 mL) pickling salt
3½ cups (875 mL) pickling vinegar (7% acetic acid)
1¼ cups (300 mL) granulated sugar
2 tbsp (30 mL) fresh thyme leaves
1 tbsp (15 mL) fennel seeds
1 tbsp (15 mL) celery seeds

If still attached, cut off and discard the fennel stalks. Rinse the bulbs under cool running water. Slice off and discard the root end. (There is no need to remove the outer layer of the bulb.) Finely chop or coarsely grate the fennel (you should have 8 cups/2 L of finely chopped or grated fennel). Add the fennel and onion to a large colander lined with a double layer of cheesecloth. Gently stir in the salt. Let the veggies drain, in the sink or over a large bowl, for 1 hour.

Rinse the veggies well under cool running water. Gather up the edges of the cheesecloth and press firmly to squeeze out excess liquid. Transfer the veggies to a large, heavy-bottomed pot. Stir in the vinegar, sugar, thyme, fennel seeds and celery seeds. Bring to a boil over high heat, stirring frequently. Reduce the heat to medium and continue cooking, stirring frequently, for 10 minutes. Remove from the heat.

Ladle into 4 clean 500 mL (2 cup) jars, leaving a ½-inch (1 cm) headspace. Poke a non-metallic utensil inside each jar a few times to remove any air bubbles, topping up the relish if needed. Process in a boiling water bath canner for 15 minutes following the Processing Checklist on page 17.

TIP Fennel stalks and fronds are also edible. If you wish, snip off some of the feathery fronds and add them to the pot with the rest of your relish ingredients. The leftover stalks can be diced and used in place of celery in soups and stews.

CHUTNEYS

When something good happens, everyone wants to be a part of it. Originating in South Asian cuisine, chutneys have been adopted around the world for their satisfying sweet and sour flavour that works with everything from roasted meats and burgers to curries and cheeses. What qualifies as a chutney means different things to different people, sometimes depending on the region they live in. Unlike relishes, which generally involve a salting process to strip produce of its water content before it's cooked briefly for a fresh flavour and crisp texture, chutneys are cooked longer in their own juices, resulting in a tender texture with deeply concentrated flavours.

Chutney fans can be pretty serious about their favourites. Cumin-Scented Mango Chutney (page 141) is a delicious classic that goes incredibly well with curries and beef burgers. My family, especially my mom and dad, also love the sweet and sour spiced flavour of Curried Apple Chutney (page 145) with turkey burgers, and Spiced Pear Cranberry Chutney (page 142) is a favourite around the holidays. The house smells incredibly inviting when a pot of chutney is simmering on the stove.

CUMIN-SCENTED MANGO CHUTNEY
SPICED PEAR CRANBERRY CHUTNEY • CURRIED APPLE CHUTNEY
PEACH CHUTNEY WITH GARAM MASALA • FOUR-ORCHARD CHUTNEY
RED WINE CHERRY CHUTNEY • FIVE-SPICE PLUM CHUTNEY
RHUBARB RAISIN CHUTNEY • SWEET THAI CHILI CHUTNEY

Cumin-Scented Mango Chutney

Fill your kitchen with the exotic scent of mango chutney spiced with cumin and mustard seeds. Serve with aromatic Indian dishes or bring out a jar at barbecue time to spoon on grilled burgers and chicken.

MAKES FIVE 250 ML (1 CUP) JARS

2 cups (500 mL) diced yellow onion
½ tsp (2 mL) salt
1 tbsp (15 mL) cumin seeds
1 tbsp (15 mL) mustard seeds
6 cups (1.5 L) diced mango (about 4 large mangoes)
3 cups (750 mL) red wine vinegar
1½ cups (375 mL) granulated sugar
1 tsp (5 mL) grated fresh ginger

Warm a large, heavy-bottomed pot over medium heat. Add the onions and the salt to the dry pot and cook for a couple of minutes, just until beginning to soften. Stir in the cumin and mustard seeds. Gently cook a couple of minutes longer, stirring frequently, without browning the onions.

Stir in the diced mango, vinegar, sugar and ginger. Bring to a boil over high heat. Maintain a hard boil for 15 minutes, stirring often, until your chutney reaches the desired consistency. Remove from the heat.

Ladle into 5 clean 250 mL (1 cup) jars, leaving a ½-inch (1 cm) headspace. Poke a non-metallic utensil inside each jar a few times to remove any air bubbles, topping up the chutney if needed. Process in a boiling water bath canner for 15 minutes using the Processing Checklist on page 17.

TIP Choose mangoes by their feel rather than by their colour. As with peaches, choose mangoes that are heavy and firm but give slightly when pressed. The mangoes can be diced a few days ahead of time and stored in a sealed container in the fridge.

SPICED PEAR CRANBERRY CHUTNEY

Firm pears simmered in cider vinegar with dried cranberries and bold spices make for a gorgeous chutney. Since pears are commonly available throughout the year, this chutney can be made any time at all, and it makes a lovely holiday gift for special friends. Try it on leftover turkey sandwiches.

MAKES SIX 250 ML (1 CUP) JARS

2 lb (900 g) firm pears
1½ lb (675 g) yellow onions, diced
2 garlic cloves, crushed
2 cups (500 mL) brown sugar
1 cup (250 mL) dried cranberries
1½ tsp (7 mL) salt
1 tsp (5 mL) ground cumin
1 tsp (5 mL) ground coriander
½ tsp (2 mL) cayenne pepper
½ tsp (2 mL) cinnamon
3 cups (750 mL) cider vinegar

Remove and discard the pear peels and cores. Dice the pears, adding them to a large, dry heavy-bottomed pot. Stir in the onions. Cook over medium heat for 5 minutes just to soften.

Stir in the garlic, brown sugar, cranberries, salt, cumin, coriander, cayenne, cinnamon and vinegar. Bring to a boil over high heat. Lower the heat to medium and simmer, stirring occasionally, for 30 to 35 minutes, until thickened. Remove from the heat.

Ladle into 6 clean 250 mL (1 cup) jars, leaving a ½-inch (1 cm) headspace. Poke a non-metallic utensil inside each jar a few times to remove any air bubbles. Process in a boiling water bath canner for 15 minutes using the Processing Checklist on page 17.

TIP While tender ripe pears are ideal for making jam, firm pears are ideal for this recipe, as they hold their shape nicely and sweeten up while cooking.

Curried Apple Chutney

Bits of sweet apple and aromatic curry come together in this sweet and tart chutney dotted with tender raisins and yellow mustard seeds. Try it with grilled turkey burgers or spread inside cold chicken sandwiches. If you're looking for a chutney with maximum flavour under the lid, this is it.

MAKES SIX 250 ML (1 CUP) JARS

3 lb (1.4 kg) apples
2 cups (500 mL) diced yellow onion
2 cups (500 mL) cider vinegar
½ cup (125 mL) malt vinegar
2 cups (500 mL) brown sugar
1 cup (250 mL) raisins
3 tbsp (45 mL) curry powder
2 tbsp (30 mL) yellow mustard seeds
1 tsp (5 mL) cinnamon

Remove and discard the apple peels and cores. Dice the apples. In a large, heavy-bottomed pot, combine the diced apple, onion, cider vinegar, malt vinegar, brown sugar, raisins, curry powder, mustard seeds and cinnamon. Bring to a boil over high heat. Lower the heat to medium and continue cooking, covered and stirring occasionally, for about 30 to 35 minutes, until the liquid has reduced and the chutney has darkened. Remove from the heat.

Ladle into 6 clean 250 mL (1 cup) jars, leaving a ½-inch (1 cm) headspace. Remove any air bubbles by poking a non-metallic utensil into each jar, spooning in more chutney if needed. Process in a boiling water bath canner for 15 minutes using the Processing Checklist on page 17.

TIP Choose apples that will hold their shape nicely when cooked, such as Granny Smith, Braeburn or Honeycrisp.

Peach Chutney with Garam Masala

Make the most of juicy summertime peaches with this simple and delicious fruit chutney. Enjoy with homemade curries or as a sweet and tangy complement to sandwiches and just about anything off the grill such as poultry, fish or slices of marinated eggplant.

MAKES SEVEN 250 ML (1 CUP) JARS

3 lb (1.4 kg) ripe peaches
3 cups (750 mL) finely diced yellow onion
1 cup (250 mL) finely diced red bell pepper
1¼ cups (300 mL) packed brown sugar
2 tbsp (30 mL) garam masala
1 tsp (5 mL) grated fresh ginger
2½ cups (625 mL) cider vinegar

With a sharp knife, score an X in the bottom of each peach. Submerge the peaches in a large pot of boiling water for 1 minute, then transfer immediately with a slotted spoon to a large bowl of cold water. Slip off and discard the skins. Holding each peach over a large, heavy-bottomed pot, tear open the fruit and discard the pits. (If using clingstone peaches, you'll need to cut out the pits with a knife.) Crush the peaches with a masher in the pot.

Stir in the onion, red pepper, brown sugar, garam masala, ginger and vinegar. Bring the works to a boil over high heat, stirring frequently. Reduce the heat to medium and simmer, uncovered and stirring occasionally, for 40 to 45 minutes, until thickened. Remove from the heat.

Ladle into 7 clean 250 mL (1 cup) jars, leaving a ½-inch (1 cm) headspace. Remove any air bubbles by poking a non-metallic utensil into each jar a few times, topping up the chutney if needed. Process in a boiling water bath canner for 15 minutes using the Processing Checklist on page 17.

TIP Hard, unripe peaches are difficult to peel. Instead, use juicy ripe peaches that give a little when pressed. If some of your peaches ripen earlier than others, store them in the refrigerator and leave the rest a day or two longer to ripen at room temperature. Garam masala is an aromatic blend of spices found in most supermarkets and South Asian food stores. Different blends are available, but the common spices are coriander, cumin, cardamom and cloves.

FOUR-ORCHARD CHUTNEY

Orchards remind us that good things really do grow on trees. Combine four orchard favourites—apples, pears, cherries and peaches—for this dark and delicious chutney. Then spread in cold chicken sandwiches, go find an orchard and have a picnic.

MAKES SEVEN 250 ML (1 CUP) JARS

2 cups (500 mL) peeled and diced apple
2 cups (500 mL) peeled and diced pear
2 cups (500 mL) pitted and chopped sweet cherries
2 cups (500 mL) peeled, pitted and diced peach
2 cups (500 mL) diced yellow onion
2 cups (500 mL) brown sugar
2 cups (500 mL) cider vinegar
2 cups (500 mL) malt vinegar
2 tsp (10 mL) ground cumin

In a large, heavy-bottomed pot, combine the apple, pear, cherries, peach and onion. Stir in the brown sugar, cider vinegar, malt vinegar and cumin. Bring to a boil over high heat. Reduce the heat to medium and simmer, uncovered and stirring occasionally, for 45 minutes or until thickened and darkened. Remove from the heat.

Ladle into 7 clean 250 mL (1 cup) jars, leaving a ½-inch (1 cm) headspace. Poke a non-metallic utensil inside each jar a few times to remove any air bubbles, topping up the chutney if necessary. Process in a boiling water bath canner for 15 minutes using the Processing Checklist on page 17.

TIP To peel peaches, score the bottoms with an X and immerse in boiling water for 1 minute. Transfer to cold water, then easily slip off the skins. If you don't have one or more of these fruits, substitute other orchard fruits such as plums, apricots or nectarines.

RED WINE CHERRY CHUTNEY

Dress up charcuterie and cheese platters with this sophisticated chutney made with sweet cherries and red wine. For another appetizer idea, spoon onto warm garlic crostini and top with parmesan shavings. The wine lover in your life will appreciate a jar of this chutney as a gift.

MAKES FIVE 250 ML (1 CUP) JARS
2½ lb (1.125 kg) sweet cherries, pitted and finely chopped
1 cup (250 mL) peeled and diced apple
1 garlic clove, minced
1½ cups (375 mL) red wine vinegar
1 cup (250 mL) red wine
½ cup (125 mL) brown sugar
½ tsp (2 mL) ground cumin
¼ tsp (1 mL) cinnamon

In a large, heavy-bottomed pot, stir together the cherries, apple, garlic, vinegar, wine, brown sugar, cumin and cinnamon. Bring to a boil over high heat, stirring occasionally. Reduce the heat to medium and simmer, uncovered and stirring occasionally, for 30 minutes or until thickened. Remove from the heat.

Ladle into 5 clean 250 mL (1 cup) jars, leaving a ½-inch (1 cm) headspace. Insert a non-metallic utensil inside each jar a few times to remove any air bubbles, topping up the chutney if needed. Process in a boiling water bath canner for 15 minutes using the Processing Checklist on page 17.

TIP Use whichever red wine you like best. A fruity Malbec or a peppery Shiraz are good choices.

FIVE-SPICE PLUM CHUTNEY

Simmer plump, juicy plums with fragrant five-spice powder for this fabulous and flavourful chutney. Enjoy with curries, dumplings, spring rolls—or anything at all.

MAKES FIVE 250 ML (1 CUP) JARS

5 lb (2.25 kg) plums (any variety)
1½ cups (375 mL) finely diced yellow onion
1½ cups (375 mL) cider vinegar
¾ cup (175 mL) brown sugar
1 tbsp (15 mL) five-spice powder
1½ tsp (7 mL) grated fresh ginger
½ tsp (2 mL) salt

Using a sharp knife, score an X in the bottom of each plum. Immerse the plums in a large pot of boiling water for 1 minute, then transfer immediately with a slotted spoon to a large bowl of cold water. Slip off and discard the skins. Coarsely chop the flesh, discarding the pits. In a large, heavy-bottomed pot, crush the plums with a masher until smoother but still chunky overall.

Stir in the onion, vinegar, brown sugar, five-spice powder, ginger and salt. Bring to a boil over high heat. Reduce the heat to medium and simmer, uncovered and stirring occasionally, for 60 minutes or until thickened. Remove from the heat.

Ladle into 5 clean 250 mL (1 cup) jars, leaving a ½-inch (1 cm) headspace. Process in a boiling water bath canner for 15 minutes using the Processing Checklist on page 17.

TIP Five-spice powder, also called Chinese five-spice, is a fragrant blend usually consisting of star anise, cinnamon, cloves, fennel seeds and Sichuan pepper. Look for it in the spice aisle of your grocery store or from a spice merchant.

RHUBARB RAISIN CHUTNEY

It's a happy moment each spring when the wrinkled new leaves of rhubarb poke through the garden soil. This chutney is a very special way to make use of those quick-growing stalks. Try a spoonful with crackers and cheese or alongside a Sunday roast.

MAKES SEVEN 250 ML (1 CUP) JARS

2 lb (900 g) rhubarb stalks

1½ lb (675 g) yellow onions, finely diced

2 garlic cloves, minced

1 cup (250 mL) raisins

1 cup (250 mL) brown sugar

1 cup (250 mL) granulated sugar

3 tbsp (45 mL) mustard seeds

2 tsp (10 mL) ground coriander

1 tsp (5 mL) cinnamon

1 tsp (5 mL) ground cumin

1½ cups (375 mL) malt vinegar

1½ cups (375 mL) cider vinegar

Rinse the rhubarb under cool running water. Chop into ½-inch (1 cm) pieces. Add the rhubarb to a large, heavy-bottomed pot along with the onion. Cook over medium heat for 5 minutes just to soften.

Stir in the garlic, raisins, brown sugar, granulated sugar, mustard seeds, coriander, cinnamon, cumin, malt vinegar and cider vinegar. Bring to a boil over high heat. Reduce the heat to medium and simmer, uncovered and stirring often, for 45 to 50 minutes, until thickened. Remove from the heat.

Ladle into 7 clean 250 mL (1 cup) jars, leaving a ½-inch (1 cm) headspace. Process in a boiling water bath canner for 15 minutes using the Processing Checklist on page 17.

TIP Rhubarb varies in colour from bright green to vibrant pink and deep red. The colour of your chutney will depend on the beautiful colours of your rhubarb. Freeze rhubarb when it's in season by chopping it into chunks and spreading the pieces out on a baking sheet. When frozen, pop into freezer bags or containers for canning another day.

Sweet Thai Chili Chutney

Vibrant Thai flavours like ginger, garlic, lime and lemongrass combine with sweet red bell peppers in this mildly spiced chili chutney. Use as a marinade or as a dipping sauce for grilled prawns, or mix with coconut milk for a quick and delicious sauce for stir-fried meat and vegetables.

MAKES SEVEN 250 ML (1 CUP) JARS

4 lb (1.8 kg) red bell peppers
3 bird's-eye chilies, minced
3 garlic cloves, minced
Zest of 1 lime
2½ cups (625 mL) finely chopped yellow onion
1½ tsp (7 mL) grated fresh ginger
2½ cups (625 mL) white vinegar
2 cups (500 mL) brown sugar
1 stalk of lemongrass

Rinse the bell peppers under cool running water. Pull off the stems, cut open the peppers and discard the seeds and ribs. Chop the peppers finely with a knife or in a food processor, and add them to a large, heavy-bottomed pot. Stir in the bird's-eye chilies, garlic, lime zest, onion, ginger, vinegar and brown sugar. Trim the lemongrass stalk at both ends and slice it in half lengthwise. Nestle it into the pot.

Bring the works to a boil over high heat. Reduce the heat to medium and simmer, uncovered and stirring occasionally, for 30 minutes. Remove from the heat. Discard the strips of lemongrass. If desired, make your chutney smooth by puréeing with an immersion blender.

Ladle into 7 clean 250 mL (1 cup) jars, leaving a ¼-inch (5 mm) headspace. Poke a non-metallic utensil inside each jar a few times to remove any air bubbles, topping up the chutney if needed. Process in a boiling water bath canner for 15 minutes using the Processing Checklist on page 17.

TIP Lemongrass can be tricky to find, but its aromatic citrus flavour is worth going out of your way for. If your regular grocery store doesn't carry lemongrass, try a specialty greengrocer or head to your nearest Asian food market.

Savoury Staples

Canning lets you stock your kitchen pantry with the very best quality ingredients. I love dressing up my home-cooked meals with bold and savoury flavours in jars, using them as a jumping-off point in my cooking. A jar of Sweet Chili Barbecue Sauce (page 161) poured over a pork shoulder and baked low and slow in the oven makes for an incredible pulled pork to go with fresh bakery buns and crunchy coleslaw. Bright and flavourful salsas are great for taco night toppings or poured over chicken breasts headed for the oven. I like to keep jars of Zesty Pizza Sauce (page 170) on hand for whipping up family-size pizzas or mini pita pizzas for the kids. By far the handiest pantry item in my kitchen is Canned Tomatoes (page 186), which can be the starting point for soups, stews, pasta dishes, rice dishes and more.

Stocking the pantry when vegetables are in season can be a real money saver too. By buying summer's finest tomatoes and peppers when they are at their best price, and by growing some vegetables in my own garden, I have been able to stock my pantry shelves with maximum potential for minimum expense.

Sweet Chili Barbecue Sauce • Bing Cherry Barbecue Sauce
Chipotle Apple Barbecue Sauce • Smoky Peach Barbecue Sauce
Herb and Garlic Tomato Sauce • Zesty Pizza Sauce • Tomato Ketchup
Bold Tomato Pepper Salsa • Tangy Tomatillo Salsa Verde
Spinach and Herb Chimichurri • Sweet-and-Sour Plum Dipping Sauce
Lemon Dill Mustard • Beer-Hive Grainy Mustard
Canned Tomatoes • Diced Tomatoes Seasoned Three Ways
Sliced Pickled Ginger • Pickled Garlic

Sweet Chili Barbecue Sauce

Tomatoes go from the garden to the grill in this delicious sauce of ripe tomatoes crushed and cooked down with brown sugar, malt vinegar and bold spices. Use as a marinade or brush on during grilling, then warm some more to slather on meat or poultry when it comes off the grill. Pour over a pork shoulder and bake low and slow for a fork-tender pulled pork to pile on buns.

MAKES FOUR 500 ML (2 CUP) JARS

7 lb (3.2 kg) tomatoes
1 cup (250 mL) diced yellow onion
2 garlic cloves, crushed
1½ cups (375 mL) brown sugar
1½ cups (375 mL) malt vinegar
3 tbsp (45 mL) chili powder
2 tbsp (30 mL) salt
1 tbsp (15 mL) dry mustard
1 tbsp (15 mL) cinnamon
1 tsp (5 mL) cayenne pepper

With a sharp knife, score an X in the bottom of each tomato. Submerge the tomatoes in a large pot of boiling water for 1 minute, then transfer immediately with a slotted spoon to a large bowl of cold water. (You may prefer to do this in batches.) Slip off and discard the skins. Add the tomatoes to a large, heavy-bottomed pot and crush with a masher.

Stir in the onion and garlic. Bring to a bubble over high heat. Reduce the heat to medium and simmer, uncovered and stirring occasionally, for 60 minutes.

Crush further until smooth, or use an immersion blender for an even smoother sauce. Stir in the brown sugar, vinegar, chili powder, salt, dry mustard, cinnamon and cayenne. Bring to a boil over high heat. Maintain a full boil for 10 minutes, stirring frequently. Remove from the heat.

Ladle into 4 clean 500 mL (2 cup) jars, leaving a ½-inch (1 cm) headspace. Process in a boiling water bath canner for 20 minutes using the Processing Checklist on page 17.

TIP Any tomatoes will do, but Roma/plum tomatoes are a good choice because they have fewer seeds and less moisture than other tomatoes.

BING CHERRY BARBECUE SAUCE

Cherries are cherished when in season, and this incredible grilling sauce absolutely does them justice. Light the grill and slather this fun and fruity sauce on slow-cooked ribs or chicken skewers, or toss with pulled pork for the best meal on a bun you've ever had.

MAKES FIVE 500 ML (2 CUP) JARS
5 lb (2.25 kg) tomatoes
3½ lb (1.6 kg) Bing cherries or any other sweet cherry variety
4 garlic cloves, crushed
3 cups (750 mL) diced yellow onion
2 cups (500 mL) cider vinegar
3 cups (750 mL) brown sugar
1 cup (250 mL) white vinegar
2 tbsp (30 mL) chili powder
2 tsp (10 mL) ground cumin
2 tsp (10 mL) cinnamon
1½ tsp (7 mL) salt

Using a sharp knife, score an X in the bottom of each tomato. Submerge the tomatoes in a large pot of boiling water for 1 minute, then transfer with a slotted spoon to a large bowl of cold water. (You may prefer to do this in batches.) Slip off and discard the skins. Chop the tomatoes into chunks, adding them to a large, heavy-bottomed pot.

Rinse the cherries under cool running water. Discard the stems and remove the pits. Add the cherries to the pot, along with the garlic, onion and cider vinegar.

Bring to a boil over high heat. Reduce the heat to medium-low and simmer, covered and stirring occasionally, for 30 minutes.

Purée the works using an immersion blender (or in a standard blender, working in batches). Stir in the brown sugar, white vinegar, chili powder, cumin, cinnamon and salt. Bring back up to a boil over high heat. Reduce the heat to medium and simmer, uncovered and stirring occasionally, for another 90 minutes. Remove from the heat.

Ladle into 5 clean 500 mL (2 cup) jars, leaving a ½-inch (1 cm) headspace. Process in a boiling water bath canner for 20 minutes using the Processing Checklist on page 17.

TIP Cherries love to be chilly. Keep them in the fridge for longer freshness and wash just before using. Handling juicy sweet cherries can mean red-stained hands. Try rubbing your hands with a wedge of fresh lemon to remove cherry stains, or wear disposable kitchen gloves.

CHIPOTLE APPLE BARBECUE SAUCE

Add sweet and smoky heat to grilled meats with this barbecue sauce made with sweet apples and plump tomatoes. Try it as a marinade for chicken or pork, then brush on some more during grilling. Chipotle fans will take one bite and go to sweet grilling heaven.

MAKES SIX 500 ML (2 CUP) JARS
4 lb (1.8 kg) tomatoes
4 lb (1.8 kg) apples
5 garlic cloves, crushed
1 cup (250 mL) diced yellow onion
2 cups (500 mL) cider vinegar
2½ cups (625 mL) brown sugar
2 tsp (10 mL) chipotle chili powder
½ tsp (2 mL) salt
¼ tsp (1 mL) nutmeg

With a sharp knife, score an X in the bottom of each tomato. Submerge the tomatoes in a large pot of boiling water for 1 minute, then transfer with a slotted spoon to a large bowl of cold water. (You may prefer to do this in batches.) Slip off and discard the tomato skins. Chop the tomatoes into quarters, adding them to a large, heavy-bottomed pot.

Peel and core the apples. Chop the apples into large chunks, adding them to the pot.

Stir in the garlic, onion and vinegar. Bring to a bubble over high heat. Reduce the heat to medium and simmer, covered and stirring occasionally, for 30 minutes.

Purée with an immersion blender (or a standard blender, working in batches). Stir in the brown sugar, chili powder, salt and nutmeg. Bring back up to a bubble and simmer, uncovered and stirring occasionally, for 1 hour, until thickened and darker. Remove from the heat.

Ladle into 6 clean 500 mL (2 cup) jars, leaving a ½-inch (1 cm) headspace. Process in a boiling water bath canner for 20 minutes using the Processing Checklist on page 17.

TIP Apples make beautiful barbecue sauces because of their natural juicy sweetness. Choose a saucing variety such as McIntosh, Golden Delicious or Gala that will go soft and smooth when cooked.

SMOKY PEACH BARBECUE SAUCE

Sweet and sunny peaches are right at home in this fabulous grilling sauce seasoned with flavourful smoked paprika. Standing at the stove stirring barbecue sauce takes time and patience. But, like anything with traditional barbecue, the results are always worth it. Try this smoky sauce with pork tenderloin or succulent chicken drumsticks.

MAKES FIVE 500 ML (2 CUP) JARS

4 lb (1.8 kg) ripe peaches

4 lb (1.8 kg) tomatoes

3 cups (750 mL) cider vinegar

1½ cups (375 mL) diced yellow onion

1½ cups (375 mL) granulated sugar

1 tbsp (15 mL) smoked paprika

1½ tsp (7 mL) salt

1 tsp (5 mL) turmeric

½ tsp (2 mL) cinnamon

Using a sharp knife, score an X in the bottom of each peach and tomato. Submerge the peaches and tomatoes in a large pot of boiling water for 1 minute, then transfer immediately with a slotted spoon to a large bowl of cold water. (You may prefer to do this in batches.) Slip off and discard the skins. Chop the tomatoes into quarters, adding them to a large, heavy-bottomed pot. Coarsely chop the peaches, adding them to the tomatoes and discarding the pits as you go.

Stir in the vinegar and onions. Bring to a boil over high heat. Reduce the heat to medium and simmer, uncovered and stirring occasionally, for 30 minutes.

Purée using an immersion blender (or a standard blender, working in batches). Stir in the sugar, smoked paprika, salt, turmeric and cinnamon. Return to a simmer over medium heat, allowing the sauce to reduce and thicken for 50 to 55 minutes, stirring frequently. Remove from the heat.

Ladle into 5 clean 500 mL (2 cup) jars, leaving a ½-inch (1 cm) headspace. Process in a boiling water bath canner for 20 minutes using the Processing Checklist on page 17.

TIP Smoked paprika adds deep, smoky flavour to the sauce without added heat. Peaches peel easier when ripe and juicy. Allow firm peaches to sit at room temperature for a few days until tender when pressed.

HERB AND GARLIC TOMATO SAUCE

Jars of homemade tomato sauce are one of the handiest staples in any kitchen. This recipe leaves the tomatoes slightly chunky, resulting in a rustic and versatile sauce. Use in pasta dishes, with meatballs or poured over cabbage rolls, or mix with some stock and a splash of cream for a quick and delicious creamy tomato soup.

MAKES FIVE 500 ML (2 CUP) JARS

10 lb (4.5 kg) tomatoes (ideally a plum variety such as Roma)
4 garlic cloves, crushed
1 tbsp (15 mL) dried basil
1 tsp (5 mL) dried oregano
1 tsp (5 mL) dried rosemary
1 tsp (5 mL) dried thyme
2 tsp (10 mL) granulated sugar
2 tsp (10 mL) salt
⅔ cup (150 mL) cider vinegar

With a sharp knife, score an X in the bottom of each tomato. Submerge the tomatoes in a large pot of boiling water for 1 minute, then transfer immediately with a slotted spoon to a large bowl of cold water. (You may prefer to do this in batches.) Slip off and discard the skins. Cut out and discard the firm white stem end. Gently squeeze out and discard most of the juice through the hole. Crush the squeezed tomatoes with a masher in a large, heavy-bottomed pot.

Stir in the garlic, basil, oregano, rosemary, thyme, sugar and salt. Bring to a bubble over high heat. Reduce the heat to medium and simmer, uncovered, for 45 minutes, stirring occasionally and then more frequently as time progresses.

Leave the sauce chunky, or if a smooth consistency is desired, run the sauce through a blender in batches or use an immersion blender right in the pot.

Line up 5 clean 500 mL (2 cup) jars. Pour 2 tbsp (30 mL) of cider vinegar into each jar. Ladle the sauce into the jars, leaving a ¼-inch (5 mm) headspace. Process in a boiling water bath canner for 35 minutes using the Processing Checklist on page 17.

TIP Tomatoes need a little added acid to make their pH safe for water bath canning. Cider vinegar is delicious in tomato sauces, canned or not. However, if you prefer, instead of vinegar you could use 1 tbsp (15 mL) bottled lemon juice in each jar.

ZESTY PIZZA SAUCE

Great pizza starts with the best homemade pizza sauce. Make a batch of this vibrant tomato and garlic sauce with dried herbs, then enjoy tasty homemade pizza for months to come. One jar is enough to make two medium pizzas or four kid-size pizzas.

MAKES TEN 250 ML (1 CUP) JARS

8 lb (3.5 kg) tomatoes
I large red bell pepper, seeded and coarsely chopped
6 garlic cloves, minced
3 tbsp (45 mL) dried oregano
2 tbsp (30 mL) dried basil
I tbsp (15 mL) salt
I tsp (5 mL) dried chili flakes
½ tsp (2 mL) black pepper
I cup (250 mL) cider vinegar

Using a sharp knife, score an X in the bottom of each tomato. Submerge them in a large pot of boiling water for 1 minute, then transfer immediately with a slotted spoon to a large bowl of cold water. (You may prefer to do this in batches.) Slip off and discard the skins. Coarsely chop the tomatoes, adding them to a large, heavy-bottomed pot.

Stir in the red pepper, garlic, oregano, basil, salt, chili flakes, black pepper and vinegar. Bring to a boil over high heat. Reduce the heat to medium and simmer, uncovered and stirring occasionally, for 30 minutes.

Purée using an immersion blender (or a standard blender, working in batches). Return to the heat and continue simmering for another 30 minutes, stirring occasionally, to thicken. Remove from the heat.

Ladle into 10 clean 250 mL (1 cup) jars, leaving a ¼-inch (5 mm) head-space. Process in a boiling water bath canner for 35 minutes using the Processing Checklist on page 17.

TIP Use any tomato variety you like, or even a mixture of varieties. For a spicy pizza sauce, add more chili flakes or 1 tsp (5 mL) cayenne pepper.

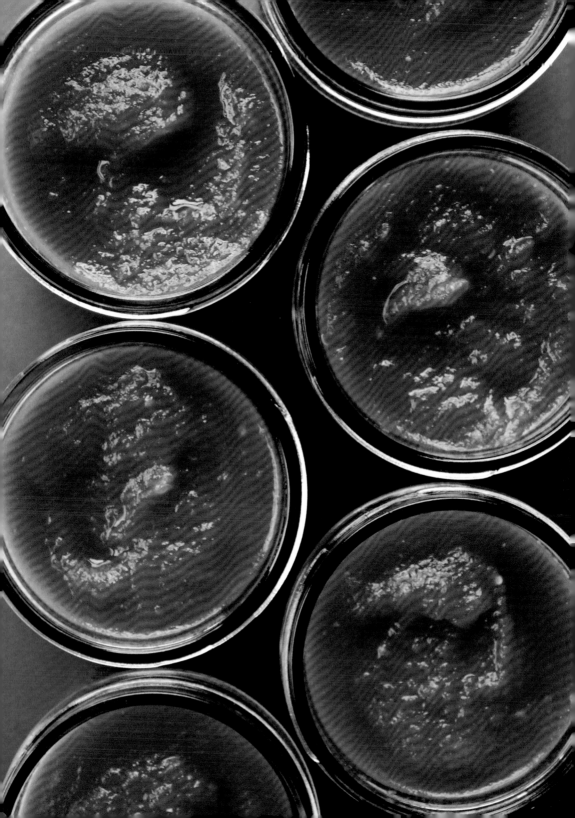

TOMATO KETCHUP

One of the most popular condiments in any kitchen, ketchup is a fun and kid-friendly project with ripe and juicy tomatoes. Making it yourself means intense tomato flavour with less sugar and salt than store-bought ketchups.

MAKES SIX 250 ML (1 CUP) JARS

8 lb (3.5 kg) tomatoes
1 cup (250 mL) diced yellow onion
3 garlic cloves, sliced
1½ cups (375 mL) white vinegar
1 tsp (5 mL) salt
1 bay leaf
¼ cup (60 mL) brown sugar

Using a knife, score an X in the bottom of each tomato. Submerge the tomatoes in a large pot of boiling water for 1 minute, then transfer immediately with a slotted spoon to a large bowl of cold water. (You may prefer to do this in batches.) Slip off and discard the skins. Cut out and discard the firm white stem ends. Gently squeeze out and discard most of the seeds through the stem end. Crush the squeezed tomatoes with a masher in a large, heavy-bottomed pot.

Stir in the onion and garlic. Bring to a boil over high heat and cook for 15 minutes, stirring frequently.

Purée using an immersion blender (or crush with a masher for a chunky ketchup). Stir in the vinegar, salt and bay leaf. Continue cooking at a gentle boil over medium heat, stirring frequently, until reduced by one half, about 60 minutes. Stir in the brown sugar about 10 minutes before the end of the cooking time. Remove from the heat and discard the bay leaf.

Ladle into 6 clean 250 mL (1 cup) jars, leaving a ¼-inch (5 mm) headspace. Process in a boiling water bath canner for 15 minutes using the Processing Checklist on page 17.

TIP For ketchup with a kick, add up to 1 tsp (5 mL) cayenne pepper or a couple of minced bird's-eye chilies to the pot during cooking.

Bold Tomato Pepper Salsa

The secret to thick home-canned salsa is to toss the veggies with a little salt to draw out the water first, then replace that water with flavours like chili powder, garlic and zingy vinegar. Grab some crunchy tortilla chips and start scooping.

MAKES SEVEN 500 ML (2 CUP) JARS

8 lb (3.5 kg) tomatoes
1½ lb (675 g) yellow onions (about 3 medium onions)
1½ lb (675 g) red bell peppers (about 3 medium peppers)
1 green bell pepper
2 tbsp (30 mL) pickling salt
4 garlic cloves, minced
1½ cups (375 mL) cider vinegar
¼ cup (60 mL) lemon juice
3 tbsp (45 mL) mild chili powder

With a sharp knife, score an X in the bottom of each tomato. Submerge the tomatoes in a large pot of boiling water for 1 minute, then transfer immediately with a slotted spoon to a large bowl of cold water. (You may prefer to do this in batches.) Slip off and discard the skins. Chop the tomatoes into 1-inch (2.5 cm) chunks, adding them to a cheesecloth-lined colander over a large bowl or in the sink.

Using a knife or food processor, finely chop the onions, red peppers and green pepper, adding them to the colander with the tomatoes. Gently stir in the salt. Let stand for 1 hour to allow the salt to draw excess moisture from the vegetables.

Without rinsing or squeezing, transfer the veggies to a large, heavy-bottomed pot. Stir in the garlic, vinegar, lemon juice and chili powder. Bring to a boil over high heat, stirring frequently. Reduce the heat to medium and simmer, stirring frequently, for 10 minutes. Remove from the heat.

Ladle into 7 clean 500 mL (2 cup) jars, leaving a ½-inch (1 cm) headspace. Poke a non-metallic utensil inside each jar a few times to remove any air bubbles, topping up the salsa if necessary. Process in a boiling water bath canner for 15 minutes using the Processing Checklist on page 17.

TIP Choose firm, ripe tomatoes for the best-tasting salsa. Prefer a fiery tomato salsa? Spice things up a bit by replacing the green pepper with 4 or 5 finely chopped jalapeño peppers. Or replace the mild chili powder with a spicy one.

TANGY TOMATILLO SALSA VERDE

Mexican food fans will love this salsa verde (green salsa) made with fresh tomatillos. The tomatillo looks like a green tomato but is in fact closely related to the cape gooseberry; both of them grow inside a husk. Enjoy with homemade enchiladas and tacos or scooped with crunchy tortilla chips.

MAKES SIX 500 ML (2 CUP) JARS

6 lb (2.7 kg) tomatillos
2 cups (500 mL) finely chopped yellow onion
I large green bell pepper, finely chopped
2 to 3 jalapeño peppers, finely chopped
¼ cup (60 mL) pickling salt
5 garlic cloves, minced
2 cups (500 mL) cider vinegar
3 tbsp (45 mL) granulated sugar
2 tsp (10 mL) ground cumin

Pull off and discard the tomatillo husks. Scrub the tomatillos under cool running water to remove the natural sticky coating. Dice the tomatillos, adding them to a large colander lined with cheesecloth. Add the finely chopped onion, green pepper and jalapeños. Gently stir in the salt. Let stand, in the sink or over a large bowl, for 1 hour to allow the salt to draw excess moisture from the vegetables.

Rinse the veggies under cool running water. Gather up the edges of the cheesecloth and squeeze out the excess liquid. Transfer the veggies to a large, heavy-bottomed pot.

Stir in the garlic, vinegar, sugar and cumin. Bring the works to a full boil over high heat, stirring frequently. Lower the heat to medium and continue cooking for 5 minutes to soften the tomatillos. Remove from the heat.

Ladle into 6 clean 500 mL (2 cup) jars, leaving a ½-inch (1 cm) headspace. Poke a non-metallic utensil inside each jar a few times to remove any air bubbles, topping up the salsa if needed. Process in a boiling water bath canner for 15 minutes using the Processing Checklist on page 17.

TIP Stirring salt into the vegetables draws out their excess moisture. Much of the salt is rinsed away before the moisture is replaced with vinegar for a tangy and flavourful salsa verde.

Spinach and Herb Chimichurri

This simple and flavourful Argentinian green sauce is traditionally drizzled with olive oil and eaten with grilled meats and seafood, but don't stop there. Try it in pasta and rice dishes for a flavourful punch of pickled herbs and garlic.

MAKES SIX 250 ML (1 CUP) JARS

1 lb (450 g) fresh spinach leaves
1 lb (450 g) fresh parsley, oregano, cilantro or basil (or a mixture)
8 garlic cloves, peeled
2 cups (500 mL) white vinegar, divided
2 jalapeño peppers, stems removed
Juice of 2 limes
2 tbsp (30 mL) pickling salt

Rinse the spinach and herbs well and pat dry with paper towel or a clean kitchen towel. Stuff half the spinach into a food processor or blender. Drop in the garlic cloves and pour in 1 cup (250 mL) of the vinegar. Pulse until smooth or very finely chopped. Stuff in the rest of the spinach and pulse again until smooth. Pour the spinach mixture into a large, heavy-bottomed pot.

Stuff half the herbs into the food processor or blender, along with the jalapeños and remaining 1 cup (250 mL) of vinegar. Pulse until smooth or very finely chopped. Stuff in the rest of the herbs and pulse again until smooth. Pour the herb mixture into the pot with the spinach mixture.

Stir in the lime juice and salt. Bring to a boil over high heat. Maintain a boil for 2 minutes, stirring constantly. Remove from the heat.

Ladle into 6 clean 250 mL (1 cup) jars, leaving a ¼-inch (5 mm) headspace. Process in a boiling water bath canner for 15 minutes using the Processing Checklist on page 17.

TIP If you buy fresh herbs and spinach by the bunch, leave the tie on and simply twist off or chop off the stems all at once. For a different chimichurri every time, mix in other leafy green herbs such as fresh mint.

Sweet-and-Sour Plum Dipping Sauce

Dress up homemade or store-bought spring rolls, chicken strips and other dipping favourites with the satisfying balance of flavours in this tasty plum sauce. A jar of this sauce makes a special homemade gift for friends who love to cook.

MAKES SIX 250 ML (1 CUP) JARS

4 lb (1.8 kg) plums
1½ cups (375 mL) diced yellow onion
3 garlic cloves, minced
2 cups (500 mL) cider vinegar
¾ cup (175 mL) granulated sugar
2 tsp (10 mL) grated fresh ginger
1½ tsp (7 mL) dried chili flakes
½ tsp (2 mL) salt

With a sharp knife, score an X in the bottom of each plum. Immerse the plums in a large pot of boiling water for 1 minute, then transfer immediately with a slotted spoon to a large bowl of cold water. Peel off and discard the skins. Coarsely chop the plums, discarding the pits.

In a large, heavy-bottomed pot, combine the plums, onion, garlic and vinegar. Bring to a boil over high heat. Reduce the heat to medium-low and simmer, covered, for 20 minutes.

Purée using an immersion blender (or a standard blender, working in batches). Stir in the sugar, ginger, chili flakes and salt. Bring to a full boil over high heat. Continue boiling over highest heat for 10 minutes, stirring frequently. Remove from the heat.

Ladle into 6 clean 250 mL (1 cup) jars, leaving a ¼-inch (5 mm) headspace. Process in a boiling water bath canner for 15 minutes using the Processing Checklist on page 17.

TIP The colour of your dipping sauce will depend on the flesh colour, not the skin colour, of your plums. Yellow, red or green flesh, choose whichever you prefer for this recipe. To make grating fibrous gingerroot easy, keep pieces of ginger in a freezer bag and grate from frozen. No peeling required!

LEMON DILL MUSTARD

Dress up grilled burgers, sausages, potato salads and more with this fabulous mustard made with the classic flavour combination of lemon and dill. Good thing it's so easy to prepare, because mustard fans will be begging for more.

MAKES FOUR 250 ML (1 CUP) JARS

¾ cup (175 mL) yellow mustard seed
2½ cups (625 mL) white vinegar
1 cup (250 mL) dry mustard
1 cup (250 mL) freshly squeezed lemon juice (about 4 large lemons)
1 tbsp (15 mL) granulated sugar
2½ tsp (12 mL) dried dillweed
½ tsp (2 mL) salt

Combine the mustard seed and vinegar in a medium saucepan. Bring to a boil over high heat. Remove from the heat, cover, and allow to stand for 2 hours to soften the seeds.

Purée the mixture in a blender until fairly smooth. Pour the mixture back into the saucepan. Stir in the dry mustard, lemon juice, sugar, dillweed and salt. Set the mixture over high heat, stirring constantly and working out any lumps with the back of the spoon. Once it comes to a bubble, remove from the heat.

Ladle into 4 clean 250 mL (1 cup) jars, leaving a ¼-inch (5 mm) headspace. Poke a non-metallic utensil inside each jar a few times to remove any air bubbles, topping up the mustard if necessary. Process in a boiling water bath canner for 15 minutes using the Processing Checklist on page 17.

TIP For even more lemon flavour, add the zest of up to 1 lemon to your mustard. Mustard needs a little time for its flavours to fully develop. Wait 1 week before opening to give your mustard time to mellow.

Beer-Hive Grainy Mustard

Make this fantastic grainy mustard with your favourite beer and sweet, golden honey. Boost your sandwiches, burgers, potato salads and more with a flavour that would please even the honey-beer himself.

MAKES FIVE 250 ML (1 CUP) JARS

1½ cups (375 mL) yellow mustard seeds
2 tsp (10 mL) brown mustard seeds
2 cups (500 mL) beer
1¼ cups (300 mL) malt vinegar
½ cup (125 mL) liquid honey
2 tbsp (30 mL) dry mustard
1 tsp (5 mL) salt

In a medium saucepan, combine the yellow and brown mustard seeds with the beer. Bring to a boil over high heat. Remove from the heat, cover, and set aside for 2 hours to soften the seeds.

Scoop the mixture into a blender. Pour in the vinegar. Purée on the highest setting until smoother (some seeds will remain whole).

Return the mixture to the saucepan. Stir in the honey, dry mustard and salt. Bring to a bubble over high heat, stirring constantly. Remove from the heat.

Ladle into 5 clean 250 mL (1 cup) jars, leaving a ¼-inch (5 mm) headspace. Poke a non-metallic utensil inside each jar a few times to remove any air bubbles, topping up the mustard if needed. Process in a boiling water bath canner for 15 minutes using the Processing Checklist on page 17.

TIP Brown mustard seed is significantly hotter than yellow mustard seed. If you like your mustard hotter, substitute some brown seed for some yellow. Wait 1 week before opening to allow your mustard to mellow.

Canned Tomatoes

The best meals start with quality ingredients—like your very own canned tomatoes. Start with a jar of these and go in any direction you like with your soups, stews, pastas, rice dishes, casseroles and more. This is a fun group canning project.

MAKES SIX 500 ML (2 CUP) JARS
6 lb (2.7 kg) tomatoes (any variety)
6 tbsp (90 mL) bottled lemon juice

Use a knife to score an X in the bottom of each tomato. Submerge the tomatoes in a large pot of boiling water for 1 minute, then transfer immediately with a slotted spoon to a large bowl of cold water. (You may prefer to do this in batches.) Slip off and discard the skins. Halve, quarter or leave the tomatoes whole.

Line up 6 clean 500 mL (2 cup) jars. Pour 1 tbsp (15 mL) lemon juice into each jar. Pack the tomatoes snugly into the jars to about 1 inch (2.5 cm) from the rim. Top up each jar with a little boiling water, leaving a ½-inch (1 cm) headspace. Poke a non-metallic utensil inside each jar a few times to remove any air bubbles, topping up with water if necessary. Process in a boiling water bath canner for 40 minutes using the Processing Checklist on page 17.

TIP While the acidity of fresh lemons changes throughout stages of ripeness, bottled lemon juice has standardized acidity. Use bottled lemon juice rather than fresh in this recipe for safe and reliable acidity in your jars. Roma tomatoes, a variety of plum tomatoes, are my favourite for canning because they are firm, with less "guts" inside. But any tomato variety can be canned using this recipe.

Diced Tomatoes Seasoned Three Ways

Making a wholesome meal in a short amount of time is simple when you have jars of diced tomatoes in the pantry. Choose to season your tomatoes with fresh leafy herbs for Italian flavours, or go in a completely different direction with Spanish or Mexican flavours. Season each jar the same or do different seasonings in the same batch. The choice is yours, and the dishes you can make are endless.

MAKES SIX 500 ML (2 CUP) JARS
Start with
7 lb (3.2 kg) tomatoes (any variety)
6 tbsp (90 mL) bottled lemon juice

For Italian diced tomatoes, add (per jar)
6 leaves of fresh basil, sage, parsley or cilantro
½ tsp (2 mL) minced garlic

For Spanish diced tomatoes, add (per jar)
¼ tsp (1 mL) smoked paprika
¼ tsp (1 mL) cayenne pepper

For Mexican diced tomatoes, add (per jar)
1 tsp (5 mL) minced jalapeño pepper
¼ tsp (1 mL) chili powder

Score an X in the bottom of each tomato. Submerge the tomatoes in a large pot of boiling water for 1 minute, then transfer immediately with a slotted spoon to a large bowl of cold water. Slip off and discard the skins. (You may prefer to do this in batches.) Dice the tomatoes, adding them to a large, heavy-bottomed pot.

Line up 6 clean 500 mL (2 cup) jars. Add 1 tbsp (15 mL) lemon juice to each jar. If desired, add your chosen seasonings to your jars.

Bring the tomatoes to a boil over high heat, stirring gently with the handle end of a wooden spoon. Remove from the heat.

Ladle the hot tomatoes into your jars, leaving a ½-inch (1 cm) headspace. Poke a non-metallic utensil inside each jar a few times to remove any air bubbles, topping up the tomatoes if necessary. Process in a boiling water bath canner for 40 minutes using the Processing Checklist on page 17.

TIP Sometimes tomatoes will float above their juices in your cooled jars. The contents are still perfectly safe and delicious.

SLICED PICKLED GINGER

Fresh gingerroot is adored for its vibrant, zingy flavour and its versatility in both savoury and sweet dishes. Pinch some of this shaved pickled ginger from the jar and mince to add to homemade stir-fries, soups and curries. A jar of this preserve makes a lovely gift for friends who like to make homemade sushi.

MAKES FIVE 125 ML (½ CUP) JARS

1 lb (450 g) fresh ginger
2 tbsp (30 mL) pickling salt
1½ cups (375 mL) white vinegar
2 tbsp (30 mL) granulated sugar

Using the side of a metal spoon, peel the ginger, discarding the skins. Slice the ginger very thinly using a mandoline or a sharp knife. Toss with the salt in a medium bowl and set aside for 1 hour.

Rinse the ginger well and drain. Combine the ginger, vinegar and sugar in a large saucepan. Bring to a boil over high heat to dissolve the sugar, then remove from the heat.

Using a slotted spoon, scoop the ginger into 5 clean 125 mL (½ cup) jars. Top up with the cooking liquid, leaving a ¼-inch (5 mm) headspace. Remove any air bubbles by poking a non-metallic utensil inside each jar a few times. Process in a boiling water bath canner for 15 minutes using the Processing Checklist on page 17.

TIP Fresh ginger is inexpensive and available year-round, making this a fun practice project for a first-time pickler. Choose firm pieces of ginger with snug, unwrinkled skins.

Pickled Garlic

These treats are less potent than fresh garlic. Pluck them from the jar to enjoy with marinated olives and vegetables or add to your cooking wherever garlic is needed. Pickle whole cloves plain or choose from three fun seasoning options. One bite of pickled garlic and the naked stuff doesn't quite seem the same again.

MAKES FOUR 250 ML (1 CUP) JARS
Start with
4 cups (1 L) peeled garlic cloves (about 1½ lb/675 g garlic bulbs)
2 cups (500 mL) white wine vinegar
1 tbsp (15 mL) pickling salt

For Tuscan pickled garlic, add (per jar)
1 fresh or dried bay leaf
1 slice of lemon

For Provençal pickled garlic, add (per jar)
1 sprig of fresh rosemary
½ tsp (2 mL) fresh or dried thyme

For Andalusian pickled garlic, add (per jar)
1 fresh or dried chili pepper
½ tsp (2 mL) black peppercorns

Rinse the garlic cloves under cool running water to remove any stray skins, then set aside.

To make the brine, bring the vinegar and salt to a boil in a small saucepan. Remove from the heat.

Add your chosen seasonings to 4 clean 250 mL (1 cup) jars. Fill the jars with the garlic cloves to about ½ inch (1 cm) from the rim. Ladle the brine over the garlic, leaving a ¼-inch (5 mm) headspace. Process in a boiling water bath canner for 15 minutes using the Processing Checklist on page 17.

TIP Peel garlic cloves quickly by putting them in a metal bowl, then invert a second metal bowl on top and shake vigorously. Or invest in a simple but effective silicone tube garlic peeler.

SWEET STAPLES

Jams, jellies and marmalades are always popular canning projects, yet there is a world of sweet preserves that don't require getting a gel set. Fruit sauces and other sweet staples are handy preserves to keep in the pantry for quick snacks and simple, last-minute desserts.

A favourite sweet staple in my house is applesauce. Both the naturally sweetened Applesauce Fruit Blends (page 197) and Cinnamon Brown Sugar Applesauce (page 198) are handy for packed lunches and useful as a top-up whenever I'm short on mashed banana for muffins and loaves. When putting together a last-minute dinner party, desserts are quick and easy with ice cream toppings such as Salted Caramel Pear Butter (page 206) and Strawberry Sundae Sauce (page 217). For something more sophisticated, it doesn't get more delicious or show-stopping than Pear Amaretto Sauce (page 209) spooned over slices of cheesecake—a personal favourite of mine.

I could go on and on about how much I love these sweet staples and how convenient they are in my pantry. The more preserves you have on hand, the more creative you can be with the homemade flavours coming out of your kitchen.

APPLESAUCE FRUIT BLENDS • CINNAMON BROWN SUGAR APPLESAUCE
SPICED APPLE TOPPING • APPLE BUTTER • APPLE PIE FILLING
SALTED CARAMEL PEAR BUTTER • PEAR AMARETTO SAUCE • PEAR SLICES
PLUM RUM RAISIN SAUCE • ORANGE CRANBERRY SAUCE
STRAWBERRY SUNDAE SAUCE • BLUEBERRY SAUCE
COUNTRY PEACH COBBLER TOPPING • PEACH SLICES
APRICOT HALVES • VANILLA BEAN STEWED RHUBARB • PINEAPPLE CHUNKS
GREEN TEA LEMONADE CONCENTRATE • CHERRY SODA SYRUP

Applesauce Fruit Blends

With no added sugar, these healthy fruit-blended applesauces are ideal for snack time and packed lunches. Choose from three delicious flavour combinations: apple blueberry, apple strawberry or apple peach.

MAKES SIX 500 ML (2 CUP) JARS
Start with
7 lb (3.2 kg) saucing apples, such as McIntosh, Spartan or Gala
4 cups (1 L) water

Choose 1 of the following
3 cups (750 mL) blueberries
4 cups (1 L) whole strawberries, hulled
2½ lb (1.125 kg) peaches (unpeeled), pitted and chopped

Rinse the apples under cool running water. Chop into quarters and add them—skins, seeds and all—to a large, heavy-bottomed pot. Pour in the water. Add your chosen blending fruit. Set over high heat and bring to a boil, then boil for 10 minutes, stirring occasionally. Reduce the heat to medium and continue cooking, stirring occasionally, for 30 to 35 minutes, until all the apples are completely soft.

Run the mixture through a food mill or conical sieve to purée the sauce and remove the skins, seeds and cores.

Ladle the sauce into 6 clean 500 mL (2 cup) jars, leaving a ½-inch (1 cm) headspace. Process in a boiling water bath canner for 15 minutes using the Processing Checklist on page 17.

TIP If you don't have a food mill or conical sieve, peel the apples and remove the cores before adding the apples to the pot. Once cooked, make the sauce smooth by using a masher or an immersion blender right in the pot.

Cinnamon Brown Sugar Applesauce

My grandmother used to make me homestyle applesauce with brown sugar and cinnamon, and it was better than any candy childhood had to offer. Enjoy this sauce in packed lunches, use in baking or grab a spoon and enjoy straight from the jar when no one's looking.

MAKES FIVE 500 ML (2 CUP) JARS
8 lb (3.5 kg) saucing apples, such as McIntosh, Spartan or Golden Delicious
1½ cups (375 mL) water
½ cup (125 mL) brown sugar
2½ tsp (12 mL) cinnamon

Remove and discard the apple peels and cores. Coarsely chop the apples, adding them to a large, heavy-bottomed pot. Pour in the water. Bring to a boil over high heat. Lower the heat to medium and cook, covered and stirring occasionally, for about 20 minutes or until the apples are fully broken down. Remove from the heat. Smooth the sauce with a masher, if desired. Stir in the brown sugar and cinnamon.

Ladle into 5 clean 500 mL (2 cup) jars, leaving a ½-inch (1 cm) headspace. Process in a boiling water bath canner for 15 minutes using the Processing Checklist on page 17.

TIP If you like your applesauce less sweet, reduce or even leave out the brown sugar. Or, if you like it sweeter, add a little extra. This applesauce is a handy top-up when you're a little short on mashed banana when making muffins or banana bread.

SPICED APPLE TOPPING

Indulge in one of fall's best flavours year-round with this chopped apple topping spiced with cinnamon, nutmeg and cloves. Use in tarts, or stir a couple of spoonfuls into a bowl of steaming oatmeal for a comforting breakfast that tastes like apple pie.

MAKES SIX 250 ML (1 CUP) JARS

1 cup (250 mL) cold water
2 tbsp (30 mL) lemon juice
3 lb (1.4 kg) firm apples, such as Granny Smith
2 tsp (10 mL) cinnamon
½ tsp (2 mL) nutmeg
½ tsp (2 mL) ground cloves
4 cups (1 L) granulated sugar

Combine the water and lemon juice in a large, heavy-bottomed pot. Remove and discard the apple peels and cores. Dice the apples, adding them to the lemon water as you go. Stir in the cinnamon, nutmeg and cloves. Bring to a full boil over highest heat, stirring frequently. Maintain a full boil for 3 to 4 minutes, until the apples begin to soften.

Stir in the sugar. Return to a full boil for 2 minutes. Remove from the heat.

Ladle into 6 clean 250 mL (1 cup) jars, leaving a ½-inch (1 cm) headspace. Poke a non-metallic utensil inside each jar a few times to remove any air bubbles, topping up with apple mixture if necessary. Process in a boiling water bath canner for 15 minutes using the Processing Checklist on page 17.

TIP Any apple will do, but if you prefer a chunky topping, choose firm apples that will hold their shape well when cooked, such as Granny Smith, Braeburn and Honeycrisp. Keep an eye out for untended apple trees in your area. In the fall, a neighbour may be thrilled to let you pick their tree in exchange for a few jars of the homemade preserves you'll make.

APPLE BUTTER

Apple butter is a timeless canning favourite. Enjoy it spread on hot cinnamon toast, or try snuggling it between two slices of buttered bread with sharp Cheddar and pan-fry for a grilled cheese experience you won't soon forget.

MAKES FIVE 250 ML (1 CUP) JARS

5 lb (2.25 kg) saucing apples, such as McIntosh, Spartan or Golden Delicious
2 cups (500 mL) water
1½ cups (375 mL) brown sugar
2 tsp (10 mL) cinnamon
½ tsp (2 mL) ground cloves
½ tsp (2 mL) nutmeg

Remove and discard the apple peels and cores. Chop the apples into large chunks, adding them to a large, heavy-bottomed pot. Pour in the water and bring to a boil over high heat. Reduce the heat to medium and continue cooking, covered and stirring occasionally, for 20 minutes or until soft.

Smooth out the sauce with a masher (or use an immersion blender for an even smoother apple butter). Stir in the brown sugar, cinnamon, cloves and nutmeg. Simmer on medium-low, uncovered and stirring frequently to prevent scorching, for 90 minutes, until dark and thick. Remove from the heat.

Ladle into 5 clean 250 mL (1 cup) jars, leaving a ¼-inch (5 mm) headspace. Poke a non-metallic utensil inside each jar a few times to remove any air bubbles, topping up with apple butter if necessary. Process in a boiling water bath canner for 15 minutes using the Processing Checklist on page 17.

TIP Experiment with other apple-friendly spices such as star anise, allspice, ginger and mace.

Apple Pie Filling

Making homemade desserts is as easy as pie when jars of this classic and comforting filling are in the pantry. This delicious filling isn't limited to just pies. It's also ideal for making apple crumble, cobbler, crisp and brown betty.

MAKES TWO 1 L (4 CUP) JARS OR FOUR 500 ML (2 CUP) JARS

2 tbsp (30 mL) lemon juice
5 lb (2.25 kg) pie apples, such as Gala or Granny Smith
1½ cups (375 mL) granulated sugar
2 tsp (10 mL) cinnamon
½ tsp (2 mL) ground cloves
½ tsp (2 mL) nutmeg

Pour the lemon juice into a large bowl and fill halfway with cold water. Remove and discard the apple peels and cores. Slice the apples about ⅛-inch (3 mm) thick, immersing the slices in the lemon water as you go to prevent browning.

In a large, heavy-bottomed pot, combine the sugar, cinnamon, cloves and nutmeg. Scoop the apples out of the lemon water and into the pot. Add ⅓ cup (75 mL) of the lemon water. Stir to coat the apples with the spices. Bring to a full boil over high heat. Reduce the heat to medium and continue cooking, tossing gently with two wooden spoons, for 2 minutes, just to soften the apples. Remove from the heat.

Pack the apples snugly into 2 clean 1 L (4 cup) jars or 4 clean 500 mL (2 cup) jars.

Bring the cooking liquid back to a boil over high heat. Maintain a full boil for 1 minute, stirring constantly, to thicken. Pour the cooking liquid over the apples, leaving a 1-inch (2.5 cm) headspace. Poke a non-metallic utensil inside each jar a few times to remove any air bubbles, topping up with more cooking liquid if necessary. Process in a boiling water bath canner for 25 minutes using the Processing Checklist on page 17.

TIP Play around with spices like ginger or allspice to find the blend you like best. To use as pie filling, pour the contents of a 1 L (4 cup) jar or two 500 mL (2 cup) jars into a large bowl. In a small bowl, mix together 2 tbsp (30 mL) cornstarch and 2 tbsp (30 mL) water. Stir the mixture into the apple filling. Pour into a double-crust pie shell and bake at 375°F (190°C) for 50 to 60 minutes, until the filling is bubbling.

Salted Caramel Pear Butter

This decadent pear butter proves that dynamic flavour can come from just a handful of simple ingredients. Slow cooking turns pears, brown sugar, lemon juice and salt into a deeply coloured, sophisticated dessert sauce. Spread this between cake layers or spoon over vanilla ice cream.

MAKES SIX 250 ML (1 CUP) JARS

8 lb (3.5 kg) ripe pears
2 cups (500 mL) brown sugar
2 tbsp (30 mL) lemon juice
1 tsp (5 mL) salt

Rinse the pears under cool running water. Remove and discard the stems, peels and cores. Dice the pears, adding them to a large, heavy-bottomed pot. Crush with a masher. Bring to a bubble over high heat. Lower the heat to medium and continue cooking for 10 minutes, stirring frequently.

Purée the pears using an immersion blender or standard blender. Stir in the brown sugar and lemon juice. Return to medium heat and let bubble for 80 to 90 minutes, stirring occasionally, until darkened and thick. (You may need to lower the heat to medium-low and stir more frequently toward the end to prevent scorching.) Remove from the heat. Stir in the salt.

Ladle into 6 clean 250 mL (1 cup) jars, leaving a ¼-inch (5 mm) headspace. Process in a boiling water bath canner for 15 minutes using the Processing Checklist on page 17.

TIP Any pear variety can be used to make pear butter, so use your favourites. Bartlett and Anjou are nice choices. To know if your pears are ripe, just check the neck. A ripe pear will give slightly when pressed just below the stem.

PEAR AMARETTO SAUCE

Amaretto liqueur lifts a batch of pear preserves from simple to sophisticated. This luxurious topping is easy to prepare and absolutely glorious spooned over vanilla ice cream or a slice of rich, creamy cheesecake. A flavour combination that's just meant to be, this is my all-time favourite thing to make with pears.

MAKES FIVE 250 ML (1 CUP) JARS

3 lb (1.4 kg) ripe pears
3 cups (750 mL) granulated sugar
½ cup (125 mL) amaretto liqueur

Rinse the pears under cool running water. Remove and discard the peels, stems and cores. Coarsely chop the pears, adding them to a large, heavy-bottomed pot. Crush with a masher into a chunky consistency.

Stir in the sugar. Bring to a full boil over highest heat, stirring frequently. Maintain a full boil for 3 to 4 minutes, until the bits of pear are tender. Stir in the amaretto. Return to a full boil for 1 minute. Remove from the heat.

Ladle into 5 clean 250 mL (1 cup) jars, leaving a ¼-inch (5 mm) headspace. Process in a boiling water bath canner for 15 minutes using the Processing Checklist on page 17.

TIP To get the best flavour from pears, allow them to ripen before using. A ripe pear should be juicy and soft instead of crunchy. To ripen hard pears, leave them at room temperature for a few days and check them again for a tender neck.

PEAR SLICES

Fresh fruit is wonderful, but canned fruit is also a huge hit in my house, especially with my kids. Canned pears are handy for adding to muffins, making quick desserts or enjoying just as they are.

MAKES SIX 500 ML (2 CUP) JARS
12 cups (3 L) water, divided
⅓ cup (75 mL) lemon juice
6 lb (2.7 kg) ripe pears
1¾ cups (425 mL) granulated sugar

In a large bowl, combine 6 cups (1.5 L) of the water with the lemon juice. Peel 1 pear. Cut in half lengthwise and remove the core (a melon baller is handy for this job), the stem and any other leathery bits. Slice the pear lengthwise, adding the slices to the lemon water as you go to prevent browning. Prepare the rest of the pears in the same manner.

In a large, heavy-bottomed pot, combine the remaining 6 cups (1.5 L) of water with the sugar. Bring to a boil to dissolve the sugar. Drain the lemon water from the pears. Add the pears to the light syrup and bring the works back up to a boil, gently stirring occasionally. Remove from the heat.

Using a slotted spoon, scoop the pears into 6 clean 500 mL (2 cup) jars, topping up with the light syrup to leave a ½-inch (1 cm) headspace. Poke a non-metallic utensil inside each jar a few times to remove any air bubbles, topping up with syrup if necessary. Process in a boiling water bath canner for 20 minutes using the Processing Checklist on page 17.

TIP The lemon juice in the soaking water prevents browning. Instead of the lemon juice, you could substitute 5 crushed 500 mg vitamin C tablets, or ½ tsp (2 mL) pure powdered ascorbic acid. Commercially available mixtures of ascorbic acid and citric acid are also available where canning supplies are sold. Follow the manufacturer's instructions on the package for mixing ratios. To avoid damaging the pears as they come to a boil, stir with the handle end of a wooden spoon.

Plum Rum Raisin Sauce

Traditional rum raisin sauce gets a fruity update with the addition of sweet, juicy plums. Try this delicious dessert sauce spooned generously over custard pies and tarts, bread puddings or scoops of ice cream.

MAKES FIVE 250 ML (1 CUP) JARS
3 lb (1.4 kg) plums (any variety)
1¾ cups (425 mL) brown sugar
1 cup (250 mL) raisins
1 cup (250 mL) rum
½ tsp (2 mL) cinnamon

Using a sharp knife, score an X in the bottom of each plum. Submerge the plums in a large pot of boiling water for 1 minute, then transfer immediately with a slotted spoon to a large bowl of cold water. Slip off and discard the skins. Chop the plums, discarding the pits as you go. Crush the plums well in a large, heavy-bottomed pot.

Stir in the brown sugar, raisins, rum and cinnamon. Bring to a boil over high heat, stirring frequently. Reduce the heat to medium and simmer, stirring frequently, for 15 minutes to thicken. Remove from the heat.

Ladle into 5 clean 250 mL (1 cup) jars, leaving a ¼-inch (5 mm) headspace. Process in a boiling water bath canner for 15 minutes using the Processing Checklist on page 17.

TIP Choose smooth, evenly coloured plums in any variety of skin and flesh colour for this recipe. They are ripe when they are tender, plump and no longer firm. Use dark rum, light rum or even coconut rum for your own one-of-a-kind sauce.

ORANGE CRANBERRY SAUCE

Let a jar of this fruity and festive cranberry sauce be the gem of your turkey dinners. Combine tart cranberries with the zest and juice of oranges for a special preserve that will have friends and relatives wanting to eat it with a spoon straight from the jar. A jar of this preserve makes a lovely hostess gift when you're invited over for turkey dinner.

MAKES FOUR 250 ML (1 CUP) JARS
6 cups (1.5 L) fresh or thawed frozen cranberries
Zest of 2 navel oranges
1½ cups (375 mL) freshly squeezed orange juice
1½ cups (375 mL) granulated sugar

Combine the cranberries, orange zest, orange juice and sugar in a large, heavy-bottomed pot. Bring to a boil over high heat. Reduce the heat to medium and continue cooking at a low boil, stirring constantly, for 10 minutes. Remove from the heat.

Ladle into 4 clean 250 mL (1 cup) jars, leaving a ¼-inch (5 mm) headspace. Process in a boiling water bath canner for 15 minutes using the Processing Checklist on page 17.

TIP Choose cranberries that are firm and bright red. Pick out and discard any bruised ones. For a festive flavour twist, add ½ tsp (2 mL) ground cloves or grated fresh ginger.

Strawberry Sundae Sauce

Grab a spoon and dig into a homemade strawberry sundae with this glorious sauce poured over scoops of vanilla ice cream. Better yet, set up a build-your-own-sundae bar with whipped cream and chopped nuts and let the whole family have fun with it.

MAKES FIVE 500 ML (2 CUP) JARS
6 lb (2.7 kg) strawberries
5 cups (1.25 L) granulated sugar

Rinse the strawberries under cool running water. Hull the berries, discarding the stems and leaves. Add the berries to a large, heavy-bottomed pot. Crush with a masher.

Stir in the sugar. Bring to a boil over high heat. Maintain a foamy boil for 10 minutes, stirring frequently. Remove from the heat. Skim off and discard the foamy pink scum.

Ladle into 5 clean 500 mL (2 cup) jars, leaving a ¼-inch (5 mm) headspace. Process in a boiling water bath canner for 15 minutes using the Processing Checklist on page 17.

TIP If you prefer larger pieces of strawberries in your sundae sauce, halve them, quarter them or even leave small ones whole. Strawberries foam up a lot while cooking, so it's important to use your largest pot and stay with your sauce so it doesn't boil over.

Blueberry Sauce

It doesn't get much better than this for blueberry fans. This silky dessert sauce dresses up a slice of creamy cheesecake or a bowl of vanilla ice cream. For breakfast, stir a heaping spoonful into yogurt or oatmeal or pour over pancakes or waffles to start the day with a heavenly blueberry experience.

MAKES FOUR 500 ML (2 CUP) JARS
3½ lb (1.6 kg) fresh or frozen blueberries (about 12 cups/3 L)
3 cups (750 mL) granulated sugar
2½ cups (625 mL) water
¼ tsp (1 mL) salt
1 tsp (5 mL) pure vanilla extract

Rinse the blueberries under cool running water, discarding any stems. Add the berries to a large, heavy-bottomed pot. Stir in the sugar, water and salt. Bring just to a boil over high heat. Reduce the heat to medium or medium-high and continue cooking at a gentle boil, stirring frequently, for 15 minutes to allow the sauce to darken a lot and thicken a little. (The sauce will thicken more as it cools.) Remove from the heat and stir in the vanilla.

Ladle into 4 clean 500 mL (2 cup) jars, leaving a ¼-inch (5 mm) headspace. Process in a boiling water bath canner for 15 minutes using the Processing Checklist on page 17.

TIP Blueberry sauce likes to set when it's left on the canning shelves, so you may need to give it a quick stir after opening.

COUNTRY PEACH COBBLER TOPPING

Country roadside diners serve some of the best desserts, like comforting peach cobbler. Spoon this dessert topping over a slice of cake or ice cream and get lost in the cinnamon-scented flavour of country peach cobbler without leaving home.

MAKES SEVEN 250 ML (1 CUP) JARS

4 lb (1.8 kg) ripe peaches
1 cup (250 mL) brown sugar
1 tsp (5 mL) cinnamon
1 tsp (5 mL) pure vanilla extract

With a sharp knife, score an X in the bottom of each peach. Submerge the peaches in a large pot of boiling water for 1 minute, then transfer with a slotted spoon to a large bowl of cold water. Slip off and discard the skins. Chop the peaches into 1-inch (2.5 cm) chunks, discarding the pits as you go.

In a large, heavy-bottomed pot, combine the chopped peaches, brown sugar and cinnamon. Bring the works to a boil over high heat, stirring frequently. Continue cooking at a full bubble, stirring frequently, for another 2 minutes. Remove from the heat. Stir in the vanilla.

Ladle into 7 clean 250 mL (1 cup) jars, leaving a ¼-inch (5 mm) headspace. Poke a non-metallic utensil inside each jar a few times to remove any air bubbles. Process in a boiling water bath canner for 15 minutes using the Processing Checklist on page 17.

TIP Ripe peaches will peel easier when using the boiling water method. Peaches that are ripe should give slightly when pressed. Hard peaches will ripen if left at room temperature for a few days.

Peach Slices

Peach season is an exciting time for home canners, and for good reason. Pure and simple, sliced peaches are one of the tastiest and most useful preserves to have in the pantry. Enjoy cold or warmed up as a quick dessert, cut up and mixed into muffins, or served over pancakes or chopped into the batter. Use the juice in marinades or in a fun and fruity cocktail.

MAKES SIX 500 ML (2 CUP) JARS
7 lb (3.2 kg) ripe peaches
4 cups (1 L) water
1 cup (250 mL) granulated sugar

With a sharp knife, score an X in the bottom of each peach. Submerge the peaches in a large pot of boiling water for 1 minute, then transfer with a slotted spoon to a large bowl of cold water. (You may prefer to do this in batches.) Slip off and discard the skins. Slice to the pit around each peach and twist in half. Discard the pits. Cut each half into about 4 slices.

In a large, heavy-bottomed pot, bring the water and sugar to a boil over high heat. Add the sliced peaches and return to a gentle boil, then remove from the heat.

Using a slotted spoon, scoop the peaches into 6 clean 500 mL (2 cup) jars, packing snugly. Top up with the cooking liquid, leaving a ½-inch (1 cm) headspace. Pop any air pockets by poking a non-metallic utensil into each jar a few times, topping up with more cooking liquid if needed. Process in a boiling water bath canner for 20 minutes using the Processing Checklist on page 17.

TIP Late-season freestone peaches are ideal for canning sliced because the pits come free from the flesh easily. Clingstone varieties can also be canned in slices, but the pits may need to be cut out or pulled away from the flesh.

Apricot Halves

Jars of canned apricots are a kid-favourite and a handy staple in the home kitchen. Chop some into pancake or muffin batter, or simply enjoy as they are straight from the jar. Two spoons, please!

MAKES SEVEN 500 ML (2 CUP) JARS

6 lb (2.7 kg) apricots
5 cups (1.25 L) water
⅔ cup (150 mL) granulated sugar
2 tbsp (30 mL) lemon juice

Rinse the apricots well under cool running water. Peel the apricots, if desired (see Tip). Slice the apricots in half, discarding the pits.

In a large, heavy-bottomed pot, combine the water, sugar and lemon juice. Bring to a boil over high heat. Add the apricot halves and return to a boil, stirring frequently. Remove from the heat.

Using a slotted spoon, fill 7 clean 500 mL (2 cup) jars equally with the apricot halves. Ladle the light syrup over the apricots, leaving a ½-inch (1 cm) headspace. Poke a non-metallic utensil inside each jar a few times to remove any air bubbles, topping up with the light syrup if needed. Process in a boiling water bath canner for 20 minutes using the Processing Checklist on page 17.

TIP To get more in each jar, pack the apricots cut side down. Skins on or skins off, it's up to you with canned apricots. If you prefer to peel them first, immerse the apricots in boiling water for 1 minute, then transfer immediately to a large bowl of cold water and slip off the skins.

Vanilla Bean Stewed Rhubarb

Old-fashioned stewed rhubarb goes from casual comfort to dazzling dessert with the addition of tiny black vanilla seeds. There's not much you can put in a jar that's tastier or more beautiful than simple stewed rhubarb.

MAKES FIVE 250 ML (1 CUP) JARS
2½ lb (1.125 kg) rhubarb stalks
1 vanilla bean
1½ cups (375 mL) granulated sugar
1 cup (250 mL) water

Rinse the rhubarb well under cool running water. Chop into ½-inch (1 cm) pieces (you should have about 9 cups/2.25 L of chopped rhubarb). Place the rhubarb in a large, heavy-bottomed pot.

Using a small sharp knife, slice the vanilla bean in half lengthwise. Using the back of the knife, scrape the length of the bean to remove the tiny black seeds. Add them to the pot, along with the vanilla bean halves.

Add the sugar and water. Bring the mixture to a bubble over high heat, stirring frequently. Reduce the heat to medium and continue cooking for 15 minutes, stirring occasionally, until the rhubarb is soft and stringy. Remove from the heat. Discard the vanilla bean halves.

Ladle into 5 clean 250 mL (1 cup) jars, leaving a ¼-inch (5 mm) headspace. Process in a boiling water bath canner for 15 minutes using the Processing Checklist on page 17.

TIP Rhubarb can be chopped and frozen for use another day. Growing your own rhubarb is easy. Buy a plant from a local garden centre and plant in a sunny spot, or ask a gardening friend for some rhubarb with plenty of attached root. Plant it in your own garden to enjoy fresh rhubarb year after year.

PINEAPPLE CHUNKS

Pineapple chunks make a simple dessert on their own or alongside cakes. For the main course, chunks of sweet pineapple elevate sweet-and-sour dishes and go nicely with pork or prawns on skewers headed for the grill. Use the juice in cocktails and marinades, or mix with sparkling water for a refreshing pineapple soda.

MAKES SIX 500 ML (2 CUP) JARS

3 large pineapples
4 cups (1 L) water
1 cup (250 mL) granulated sugar

Cut off and discard the leaves and base of each pineapple. Resting each pineapple on end, slice down the sides to remove the spiny skin, working all the way around. Slice off any remaining eyes around the pineapple. Rest each pineapple on its side and cut into 1-inch (2.5 cm) thick rounds. Chop the rounds into 1-inch (2.5 cm) chunks, discarding the tough core as you go.

Add the pineapple chunks to a large, heavy-bottomed pot. Pour in the water and sugar. Bring to a boil over high heat, stirring frequently. Reduce the heat to medium and continue cooking at a gentle boil for 8 to 10 minutes, stirring frequently, to soften the pineapple slightly. Remove from the heat.

Using a slotted spoon, scoop the pineapple equally into 6 clean 500 mL (2 cup) jars. Ladle the cooking liquid into the jars, leaving a ½-inch (1 cm) headspace. Poke a non-metallic utensil into each jar a few times to remove any air bubbles. Process in a boiling water bath canner for 15 minutes using the Processing Checklist on page 17.

TIP Although available year-round, peak season for pineapples is May through June. Smell the bottom of a pineapple. If it's floral, it's ripe and ready for canning. If it smells fermented, it has gone off. If it doesn't smell like anything, leave it at room temperature for a few days to ripen.

Green Tea Lemonade Concentrate

Open a jar of this simple concentrate to whip up a pitcher of refreshing still or sparkling green tea lemonade. Preserve this citrus concoction in winter when lemons are in season, then pour over ice and enjoy on a hot summer's day.

MAKES SEVEN 250 ML (1 CUP) JARS

2 tbsp (30 mL) green tea leaves
3 cups (750 mL) boiling water
4 cups (1 L) granulated sugar
3 cups (750 mL) freshly squeezed lemon juice

Put the tea leaves in a teapot or small saucepan. Pour the boiling water over the tea, cover, and allow to steep for 10 minutes.

Strain the tea into a large, heavy-bottomed pot, discarding the tea leaves. Add the sugar and lemon juice. Bring just to a boil over high heat. Remove from the heat.

Ladle into 7 clean 250 mL (1 cup) jars, leaving a ¼-inch (5 mm) headspace. Process in a boiling water bath canner for 15 minutes using the Processing Checklist on page 17.

TIP To get 3 cups (1 L) of juice, you'll need about a dozen lemons. On average, 1 lemon contains ¼ cup (60 mL) of juice. To reconstitute, mix 1 jar of concentrate with 6 cups (1.5 L) of still or sparkling water, or as you like it.

CHERRY SODA SYRUP

Stretch out the short sour cherry season all year long with this delicious and natural soda syrup. Mix with sparkling water or use the syrup to add a shot of cherry flavour and colour to your cocktails.

MAKES SIX 250 ML (1 CUP) JARS

1½ lb (675 g) sour cherries
5 cups (1.25 L) water
4 cups (1 L) granulated sugar

Rinse the cherries under cool running water. Pluck off and discard the stems. Add the cherries, pits and all, to a large pot. Cover with the water and bring to a boil over high heat. Reduce the heat to medium, cover, and continue cooking for 15 minutes.

Pour the mixture through a fine-mesh sieve, discarding the cherry pulp and pits.

Return the liquid to the rinsed pot. Stir in the sugar. Bring just to a boil over high heat. Remove from the heat.

Ladle into 6 clean 250 mL (1 cup) jars, leaving a ¼-inch (5 mm) headspace. Process in a boiling water bath canner for 15 minutes using the Processing Checklist on page 17.

TIP For a classic cherry soda, pour ¼ cup (60 mL) of soda syrup over ice and top with about 1½ cups (375 mL) of sparkling water, or play around to find the ratio you like best.

THANKS

Two important ingredients went into making this book: love and support. My deep gratitude to Rueben for his unwavering encouragement, extra time with the kids and for never complaining about the hundreds of mason jars in the house. Rowan and Jasper, you're just little now but you've been so good about Mommy's long hours in the kitchen. To my mom for her constant support, deep tea towel collection and the loan of family heirlooms for photographs. To the biggest fan of preserves I know, my dad, who has been training his entire life to taste-test this book. To my friends and neighbours who came home to find jars on their doorsteps and accepted preserves whenever they were offered, your enthusiastic taste-testing skills and thoughtful feedback inspired many recipe tweaks along the way. To Keri Coles for making me look good. To my food blogging sisters Julie Van Rosendaal, Jan Scott and Renée Kohlman, thank you for cheering me on. To Dan and Micayla at The London Chef for believing in me and always making room in your kitchen for simple, good home cooking. To my copy editor, Shaun Oakey, thank you for your careful eye and helpful nudges. To the talented Andrea Magyar and her team at Penguin, thank you for seeing something in me and bringing this wonderful project into my life. All of you are in the pages of this book.

INDEX

mustard
    beer-hive grainy, 185
    lemon dill, 182

N
nectarines
    and vanilla bean jam, 49

O
onions. *See also* pearl onions; red
        onions
    apple chutney, curried, 145
    Bing cherry barbecue sauce, 162
    chipotle apple barbecue sauce, 165
    corn relish, 134
    cumin mango chutney, 141
    fennel thyme relish, 137
    five-spice plum chutney, 153
    Four-Orchard Chutney, 149
    green relish, 121
    Hot Dog Relish, 125
    peach chutney with garam masala,
        146
    Rainbow Pepper Relish, 133
    rhubarb raisin chutney, 154
    and spiced pear cranberry
        chutney, 142
    sweet-and-sour plum dipping
        sauce, 181
    sweet chili barbecue sauce, 161
    sweet Thai chili chutney, 157
    tomatillo salsa verde, 177
    tomato ketchup, 173
    tomato pepper salsa, 174
    and zucchini sweet relish, 126
oranges
    blood, vanilla marmalade, 85

    and blueberry marmalade, 94
    and cranberry sauce, 214
    habanero pepper jelly, 66
    mandarin ginger marmalade, 86
    and pineapple marmalade, 97
    thick cut marmalade, 82

P
peaches
    applesauce fruit blends, 197
    chutney with garam masala, 146
    cobbler topping, 221
    Four-Orchard Chutney, 149
    jam, 50
    slices, 222
    smoky, barbecue sauce, 166
pearl onions
    pickled, 117
pears
    and amaretto sauce, 209
    and cranberry spiced chutney, 142
    Four-Orchard Chutney, 149
    and ginger jam, 45
    salted caramel butter, 206
    slices, 210
pectin, 6–7
peeler, 14
peppers. *See* green peppers; hot
        peppers; red bell peppers;
        yellow peppers
pickles
    asparagus spears, 113
    beets, 110
    bread and butter, 102, 190–93
    cabbage and onion, 114
    dill, 105
    dill beans, 106

ABOUT THE AUTHOR

Amy Bronee is a food blogger, recipe writer and cooking instructor. Millions of home cooks around the world visit her blog FamilyFeedbag.com for simple and inviting recipes and mouth-watering foodtography. Amy was named one of Western Canada's Top 40 Foodies Under 40, and among its many awards, Family Feedbag is recognized as one of Canada's top food blogs. Amy lives in Victoria, B.C., with her husband and two young boys.